Edward Hartley Dewart

Essays for the Times

Studies of Eminent Men and Important Living Questions

Edward Hartley Dewart

Essays for the Times
Studies of Eminent Men and Important Living Questions

ISBN/EAN: 9783744660471

Printed in Europe, USA, Canada, Australia, Japan

Cover: Foto ©Thomas Meinert / pixelio.de

More available books at **www.hansebooks.com**

ESSAYS FOR THE TIMES.

STUDIES OF EMINENT MEN

AND

IMPORTANT LIVING QUESTIONS.

BY

REV. E. H. DEWART, D.D.

TORONTO:
WILLIAM BRIGGS,
WESLEY BUILDINGS.
MONTREAL: C. W. COATES.   HALIFAX: S. F. HUESTIS.
1898

Entered according to Act of the Parliament of Canada, in the year one thousand eight hundred and ninety-eight, by WILLIAM BRIGGS, at the Department of Agriculture.

THE AUTHOR'S PREFACE.

EVERY author who appeals to the public to purchase and read a new book, should have a reason to give for such a demand. Some people think, because of the vast number of books already in existence, that there can be no need for publishing new books. But the literature of a country or age is the record of its thought and progressive life; and, unless all mental activity should cease, there must be a necessity for some literary expression of the thoughts of the thoughtful on subjects of living interest. Besides, it should be borne in mind that every age has its own forms of error, which require some suitable exposure or refutation in the religious literature which is provided for the people.

As every Essay in this volume was written, because the subject discussed took a special hold of my thoughts, and was felt to be a living question requiring to be studied and discussed, I have been led to think that their publication in book form would interest and help many readers, who have not had the same time and opportunity for studying these subjects.

I was confirmed in this opinion by re-reading my review of "The Life and Letters of Frederic W. Robertson," published in the *Methodist Quarterly Review*, of New York, over thirty years ago. I was gratified to find how well the views then expressed have stood the test of time, and how strikingly my opinion of the tendency of Robertson's theological views has been justified by the developments of recent years. I may venture to claim for this article that it presents an appreciative recognition of Robertson's great intellectual gifts and moral courage, while fairly pointing out some of his unsound and fanciful doctrinal theories. As Robertson's sermons are still widely read, this Essay should possess a living interest for many readers. James Arminius, the eminent Dutch theologian, is a subject of even greater interest; not merely because of his far-reaching influence on theological belief, but also because the great majority of those who hold his views of Scripture truth know very little about his noble character and stirring life-history.

In "Questionable Tendencies in Current Theological Thought," I have pointed out some exaggerations of truth, against which it is necessary to guard at the present time. "Theological Teaching in Public Schools" is a subject of special living interest. The same may be said of such questions as: "What Should Ministers Preach?" and "Is the World Growing Worse?" If the views I have presented, in answer to these and other questions discussed in this volume, are sound and scriptural, I may indulge a hope that the book will be instructive, as well as interesting, to younger ministers and other seekers after truth who read it.

The essay on Charles Sangster, and the selections from the Poems I have written since the publication of my "Songs of Life," may interest readers to whom Poetry is more attractive than Theology. As these articles were written at widely different times and for different periodicals, each Essay discusses the subject of which it treats without regard to what may have been said in any other Essay in the volume.

E. H. DEWART.

TORONTO, AUGUST, 1898

CONTENTS.

		PAGE
I.	Robertson of Brighton	7
II.	Charles Sangster, a Canadian Poet of the Last Generation	38
III.	James Arminius, the Great Dutch Theologian	52
IV.	Questionable Tendencies in Current Theological Thought	71
V.	The Tübingen School of Criticism	87
VI.	Confessions and Retractions of an Eminent Scientist	99
VII.	What Should Ministers Preach?	109
VIII.	Moral Teaching of the Old Testament	115
IX.	The Last of the Great Prophets	125
X.	Is the World Growing Worse?	155
XI.	Theology in the Public Schools	161

LATER POEMS

Written since the publication of "Songs of Life."

	PAGE
THE LONG VICTORIAN REIGN	171
TO THE CANADIAN NIGHT-HAWK	173
ON THE DEATH OF LORD TENNYSON	175
THEN AND NOW	177
OUR DEAR DEAD BOY	183
DEATH OF JOHN KEATS	187
LINES TO A PESSIMIST	190
CHRISTMASTIDE	193
THE SONG OF THE WIND	194
WILLIAM EWART GLADSTONE	197

ESSAYS FOR THE TIMES.

I.

ROBERTSON OF BRIGHTON.*

SOME men owe their chief distinction to the circumstances with which they happen to be connected. Others owe little to externals, and interest us mainly by the history of their interior life—by what they thought and felt, the development of their moral and intellectual power. There is no doubt that every thoughtful mind has an inward history, which if it could be distinctly portrayed would prove worthy of attention and study. These volumes are pre-eminently a mental history, which chains our attention by laying bare the growth, conflicts and thinkings of a gifted and impassioned soul. It is frequently said that the organized associations which occupy every department of human activity, and other features of this age, are unfavorable to the development of individuality of character. The most laudable efforts of the solitary artisan are eclipsed and superseded by the result of the combined skill and

* "Life and Letters of Frederick W. Robertson, M.A.," Incumbent of Trinity Chapel, Brighton, 1847-53. Edited by Stopford A. Brooke, M.A., late Chaplain to the Embassy at Berlin. In two volumes. Boston: Ticknor & Fields. 1865.

industry of different countries and generations. The single-handed valor of the "bravest of the brave" no longer turns the tide of battle. Whatever field of investigation we select, we discover the footprints of previous explorers, till learning has become mainly a knowledge of what others have thought and done, rather than reading new pages from the book of nature for ourselves. Yet at intervals, as if to give evidence of undiminished vigor, nature gives to the world a man of character so sharply outlined, and so unmistakably independent, that the admiration of those who are borne along by his influence and the opposition of those who are alarmed at his disregard for canonized prejudices, alike point him out as a leader among men, one who has sufficient innate strength of soul to swim against the prevailing tides and currents of the time. Such a man stands out before us in this biography.

Whatever differences of opinion may exist respecting the soundness of his theological teaching, there can be no question that Frederick W. Robertson possessed rare mental gifts which lifted him out of the ranks of ordinary men. Such intensity of feeling and vivid imagination has seldom been found in union with equal clearness of intellect and power of sustained thought on abstruse subjects. In him are blended the mental subtlety of the philosopher, the spiritual vision of the poet, and the stern decision of the earnest practical worker. Though during his life his name was quite unknown on this side of the Atlantic, and comparatively so in England, yet no sermons of our day have awakened so deep and extensive an interest as the fragmentary discourses of this Brighton curate, whose life was so sorely lacerated with the "thorns and briers of the wilderness," and who died with an oppressive feeling of failure and disappointment, shrouding like a dark shadow his worn and bleeding heart. They have stirred the hearts of thousands, both in England and America, with their burning and electric eloquence, and have probably been preached by many who have scarcely apprehended their theological standpoint, or grasped their logical tendencies. This extensive popularity of the sermons was naturally followed by a wish to know something of the author. To gratify this wish the present "Life and Letters" has been given to the public. Like most recent biographies, the work consists mainly of selections from private correspondence. It is generally conceded that from no other source can we gain so true a conception of the character of a man. This method, however, may be overdone. Either from modesty or slothfulness, modern biographers frequently keep too much in the background. If the writer of a life be really qualified for the task he undertakes, by a special acquaintance with the subject of his work, he is surely under obligations to give the advantage of his superior knowledge to his readers, and by a judicious condensation to save them the labor of wading through piles of prosy correspondence for the sake of a very little additional knowledge.

These remarks do not apply to the work before us. "Robertson, of Brighton," has been fortunate in his biographer. The letters, though fragmentary and unconnected, help us to understand a man who is certainly worth knowing. The light they reflect upon the inner life and theological opinions of their gifted author constitutes the main value of this biography. They possess a rare freshness and attraction, and give us clear glimpses into his soul's life. Every sentence throbs with life and feeling; and bears an unmistakable impress of sincerity, earnestness and independence. The portions of the work supplied by the pen of Mr. Brooke, though little more than the frame in which these fragments are set, evince superior mental grasp and culture, and a deep and appreciative admiration of Robertson's character and teaching. External events are properly only regarded in their influence on the development of his character. And although doubtless Mr. Brooke's warm admiration for the teaching and character of Robertson has led him to see everything in the most favorable light, we thankfully acknowledge the fearless candor with which he gives us letters that some would think reveal too much weakness and petulance to be published. We want to see such a man for ourselves. And we have in these volumes, taken in connection with his published sermons, the means of forming a tolerably correct estimate of the man, and of his position as a theologian.

The popularity of his sermons, and the manner in which his views are spoken of by many who claim an adherence to the standard theology of the Reformation, as well as the fact of his being in some sense a representative man, illustrating a tendency to freer thought and greater latitude of opinion in theology, warrant us in calling attention to a brief review of his life and mental history as here indicated, and of the relation of his theology to the Bible, and to those central truths which constitute the creed of evangelical Protestants.

Frederick W. Robertson was born in 1816. He was the son of a British officer, who outlived him. He owed much to the careful education and watchfulness of his parents. Even in childhood, there seems to have been nothing in external nature that did not give him pleasure and awaken a vivid interest.

He excelled in manly games and athletic exercises, and yet joined to this a love of reading and quiet remarkable for one of his age. His progress in his studies early evinced superior mental capacity. Enthusiastic admiration of a military life was early developed, and continued singularly strong to the end of his life. "I was rocked and cradled," he writes, "to the roar of artillery, and the very name of such things sounds to me like home. A review, suggesting the conception of a real battle, impresses me to tears. I cannot see a regiment manœuvre, nor artillery in motion, without a choking sensation." Application was made in his behalf to the authorities, and his name placed on the list as a candidate for a place in a cavalry regiment in India. He began to study for this prospective sphere with ardent enthusiasm. It was long before the desired appointment was conferred, and in the meantime his friends began to urge him to enter the ministry. This caused him many mental struggles and deep perplexity. But at length, after the military appointment was obtained, mainly in deference to the wishes of his father, he decided for the ministry and went to Oxford to study for orders. Here he was brought into direct contact with the Tractarian controversy; and, though rejecting the teaching of the High Church leaders of that movement, he cherished a warm admiration for many of the men of that party, which was strengthened rather than diminished by the lapse of years. His Oxford life was chiefly distinguished by its exemplary character, and by his deep sense of the responsibilities of the sacred office to which he looked forward. He was ordained in 1840, and was successively curate of Winchester and Cheltenham, which latter place he left in 1846, through causes that changed his whole future life.

During these early years of his ministry, although observant minds recognized evidences of superiority, he had not yet developed that remarkable intellectual power which arrested such general attention afterward at Brighton. The ascetic severity with which he observed the duties of religion during this period reminds us of the struggles of John Wesley, before he clearly apprehended the doctrine of justification by faith. The issue, however, was widely different. Mr. Robertson had entered the ministry a decided adherent of the Evangelical Calvinistic party in the National Church, and for some years maintained the tenets of that section.

The following quotations from his correspondence show his theological position during this period:

"I believe there is at this time a determined attack made by Satan and his instruments to subvert that cardinal doctrine of our best hopes, justification by faith alone; and how far he has already succeeded let many a college in Oxford testify. It is the doctrine which, more than any other, we find our own hearts continually turning aside from and surrendering. Anything but Christ. The Virgin, the Church, the Sacraments, a new set of resolutions—any or all of these will the heart embrace as a means to holiness or acceptance, rather than God's way."

Again, speaking of a conversation with a professed Liberal in theology at Geneva, he says:

"My chief point was to prove the death of Christ not merely a demonstration of God's willingness to pardon, on repentance and obedience, but an actual substitution of suffering; and that salvation is a thing *finished* for those who believe, not a commencement of a state in which salvation may be gained; insisting especially on Hebrews x. 14. . . . I admit that want of assurance is the mark of very low attainments in grace."

And at a still later date he writes:

"I quite agree with you about the Calvinistic doctrines. I think we ought to preach them in the proportion in which they are found in Scripture, connected always with election unto holiness."

These positions were very soon to be abandoned forever. As we pursue his history, we find him explicitly renouncing these views, and taking up a position of stern antagonism to the "Evangelicals," which at times was distinguished by an intense bitterness and aversion that must be regretted as a weakness, partly resulting from his sensitive nervous organization.

During the later years of his stay at Cheltenham he began seriously to doubt the soundness of the views he had hitherto entertained. These doubts gradually grew upon him until his soul was steeped in perplexity and the creed of his youth seemed to drift from his grasp, like a wreck swept before the relentless waves of fate.

In the latter part of 1846, on account of the failure of his health, he went again to the continent, where he remained for some months, preaching occasionally at Heidelberg, and deeply pondering the questions which now perplexed his soul with an agony of bewildering thought. Writing to a friend, he says:

"For instance, suppose a man puts the question, 'Who was Christ? What are miracles? What do you mean by inspiration? Is the resurrection a fact or a myth? What saves a man, his own character, or that of another? Is the next life individual consciousness, or continuation of the consciousness of the universe?' To these and twenty other opinions which I could put, Krause would return one answer, Neander another, and Dr. Chalmers another."

The wildness and grandeur of the scenery by which he was surrounded and the opportunity for solitary musing, afforded by relief from active duty and separation from friends, doubtless intensified the emotions which his inquiries awakened. Never, perhaps, were the struggles and doubts of a soul drifting away from the once sacred way-marks of life more vividly described than in a lecture afterward delivered in Brighton, in which he evidently portrays his own experience. Such words could only come from a soul that had felt the bewildering agony of doubt which they so vividly portray:

"It is an awful moment when the soul begins to find that the props on which it has blindly rested so long are, many of them, rotten, and begins to suspect them all; when he begins to feel the nothingness of many of the traditionary opinions which have been received with implicit confidence, and in that horrible insecurity begins also to doubt whether there be anything to believe at all. It is an awful hour—let him who has passed through it say how awful—when this life has lost its meaning and seems shrivelled into a span; when the grave appears to be the end of all, human goodness nothing but a name, and the sky above this universe a dead expanse, black with the void from which God himself has disappeared! In that fearful loneliness of spirit, when those who should have been his friends and counsellors only frown upon his misgivings and profanely bid him stifle doubts which, for aught he knows, may arise from the fountain of truth itself; to extinguish, as a glare from hell, that which, for aught he knows, may be light from heaven; and everything seems wrapped in hideous uncertainty—I know but one way in which a man may come forth from his agony scathless: it is by holding fast to those things that are certain still, the grand, simple landmarks of morality. In the darkest hour through which a human soul can pass, whatever else is doubtful, this at least is certain. If there be no God and no future state, yet even then it is better to be generous than selfish, better to be chaste than licentious, better to be true than false, better to be brave than to be a coward."

During his stay at Heidelberg he plunged deeply into German metaphysics and theology, and he returned to Cheltenham less improved in health than his friends had hoped, though calmer and more composed in mind. The work of rejecting tenets he had held on the authority of others, without feeling their truth in his own consciousness, was now tolerably complete. The positive views which distinguish his later teaching were, doubtless, more slowly evolved. Believing that "it has been given us to know our base from our noble hours; to distinguish between the voice which is from above and that which speaks from below out of the abyss of our animal and selfish nature," like a strong swimmer who has confidence in his strength he cast himself boldly into the tide of life, and parted forever from the position he once occupied. The honored term "Protestant," that had been the watchword of the Church in many a grave crisis, henceforth he strangely regards as designating only the Calvinistic Evangelism which excited his strong aversion; and hence he often charges "Protestantism" with views that the great majority of Protestants would indignantly repudiate.

Of the existence of a consistent system of theology, based on juster views of human freedom and responsibility and nobler conceptions of the breadth and fullness of divine benevolence revealed in Christ, as held by a large section of the Protestant Church, he seems to have known nothing.

As we follow him from this great turning point in his mental history, we are sometimes saddened at seeing him so impulsively and fiercely assume positions that we cannot but regard as untenable and unsafe; yet he continues to the last distinguished by high-souled manliness, profound human sympathy and unswerving fidelity to his convictions of truth.

Before returning from the continent he surrendered the curacy of Christ's Church, Cheltenham, which he had held for nearly five years. After remaining for a few months without a pastoral charge, he was appointed by the Bishop of Oxford to the curacy of St. Ebbs, Oxford. Here the eloquence and independence of his preaching were beginning to attract attention, when, with the consent of the Bishop, he accepted the perpetual curacy of Trinity Chapel, Brighton, which continued to be the scene of his labors till his death in 1853.

The year previous to his coming to Brighton was, as we have seen, the transition period in his theological views, and as he came with a fixed purpose to speak out his sentiments fearlessly, he soon awakened profound attention; like all earnest and independent preachers, securing both opposition and admiration. Many who had previously gone to no place of worship were charmed by the freshness and vigor of his sermons, and thronged his church. Thoughtful and inquiring minds for whom he had cast light upon some of the perplexing problems of theology, or at least had put a construction upon them that made them less objectionable, hung upon his words with deep and admiring interest. His friends claim for him that he was the means of bringing many Unitarians, and even Roman Catholics, into the Church. But there is certainly ground to question whether this result was not attained rather by going a long way to meet them, than by bringing them to receive the historic doctrines of the Church of England.

He displayed a deep interest in the social and mental improvement of the working classes; organizing an institute and library for their benefit, delivering lectures on social and literary topics, and courageously opposing the introduction of infidel books into the library. He was so much the soul of this movement that the institute did not survive him. Though education and natural tastes prompted him to side with the aristocracy, his liberal principles and broad human sympathies led him always to identify himself with the people, and to defend the rights and dignity of manhood. This sympathy was so deep in tone and warm in expression, that in some quarters he was charged with being in league with the Socialists and Chartists, whose errors he so fearlessly and wisely combated.

During the whole period of these Brighton labors, which encircle his name with such brilliant renown, though no longer the subject of such severe mental conflicts as those that harassed his soul at Cheltenham, his life was overshadowed by a morbid melancholy. He felt himself to be isolated by his independence from sympathy, opposed and misunderstood by former friends, a pioneer in intricate and thorny paths, without human guidance or companionship, and haunted continually by the silent but unyielding footstep of a fatal disease. While his words were voices of hope and consolation to others, he bore about with him an intensely lonely and sorrowful heart. This feeling that he was alone, misunderstood and wronged by false judgment, inspired and developed that profound sympathy with the life and character of Him who " was despised and rejected of men, a man of sorrows and acquainted with grief," and that ardent appreciation of Christ's human sympathy that is so prominent a feature in many of his sermons. It is impossible to read such sermons as that on the " Loneliness of Christ," without feeling that the pencil with which he paints so vividly has been dipped in the crimson current of his own heart. And yet this feeling was more the result of constitutional sensitiveness and melancholy, increased by intense mental application and painful disease than of any uncommon trials he had to endure at Brighton. That he was misunderstood and misrepresented is doubtless true enough. It would have been strange had it been otherwise. What independent seeker after truth ever escapes this? Some, sincerely believing his teaching to be erroneous and dangerous, left the church. This pained and grieved him exceedingly. It is to be regretted that the opposition or unfriendly criticism, which he affected to despise, should provoke such expressions of bitterness and hostility as occasionally escape him. He could not reasonably expect that people would listen quietly and approvingly to statements of doctrine which they regarded as at variance with their most cherished convictions of truth. If it cost himself such mental agony to tear himself loose from the faith of his youth, how could he suppose that others would renounce their cherished beliefs without a struggle? He was certainly sufficiently ardent and outspoken in the expression of his own opinions to have made greater allowance for the earnestness and frankness of those who differed from him. His biographer, in his intense opposition to the "Evangelicals," seems to give undue prominence to those expressions of aversion and complaint that a momentary weakness and pain may have wrung from his morbidly sensitive nature. Mr. Brooke constantly takes for granted that Robertson was right and all who differed from him or opposed him wrong; and that he was wronged and ill-used by all who did not accept his utterances as oracular. This is the intolerance of liberalism. He ought to have remembered Robertson's own words: "It seems to me a pitiful thing for any man to be true and to speak truth, and then complain in astonishment that truth has not crowns to give him but thorns." It is astonishing what forbearance some people expect. It is not enough that they are left to form their opinions independently and to express them freely without restriction. To speak against them or oppose them is stigmatized as bigotry and intolerance. Such suppression of all unfavorable criticism of opinions which we regard as false or dangerous in their tendency, is inconsistent with any real attachment to our own views, or a belief of their truth and importance. Those who are drifting about in a cloud-land of sceptical uncertainty, without any fixed religious convictions, may treat all religious principles alike. But such a course is the result of indifference, not of liberality.

There is something intensely sad in watching the progress of an unrelenting disease gaining its terrible conquests over the vital energy of his physical structure. But in Robertson's case this sadness is greatly increased by the nature of the malady (disease of the brain) which shattered his noble intellect, as well as prostrated his bodily health. He continued to work with an intensity that quickened his decline. Most of the time he suffered excruciating pain. He complains to his friends that he no longer had the capacity of thought he once consciously possessed. The refusal of the rector, on some personal grounds, to sanction the appointment of an assistant who was acceptable to Mr. Robertson and the people, gave him much anxiety and regret; and by leaving him to struggle alone with responsibilities for which he was utterly incompetent hastened his end. Amid increasing pain and feebleness we catch occasional gleams of the old intellectual fire. But the struggle rapidly hastened to its close. On Sunday, August 15th, 1853, at the age of 37, in the prime of manhood, he died. "At his own chapel that morning, when the rumor went round that there was no hope, and God was to be sought to hear the prayer for him and all sick persons, many wept bitterly; but the greater part of those who loved and venerated him were stunned beyond the power of weeping."

In following the course of Robertson's outward history we discover no exceptional distinction that separates him from his contemporaries. Many, whom oblivion enshrouds in her impenetrable shades, have passed through similar struggles, successes and sorrows. It is the light cast back upon his life by the blaze of fame and popularity kindled by the publication of his sermons, a few years after his death, that invests the incidents of his life and mental growth with such uncommon interest. He vindicates his rights to be enrolled with the gifted sons of genius, by the fact that at the point where common names grow dim and pass away from sight forever, his only begins to gather around it a deeper interest and to shine with clearer and more enduring light. In the history of the British pulpit no similar productions (left by their author without a thought of publication) have secured equal attention. What is the secret of this influence? To all thoughtful minds his deep though subdued earnestness, his singular felicity of illustration, his glowing imagination, flashing light on the obscure and giving life and form to the abstract, his clear musical voice, " which seldom rose, but when it did, yielded a rich volume of sound toned like a great bell," and the force and beauty of his thoughts, must have made him, in the best sense of the terms, popular and attractive as a preacher. But all this would not fully account for the interest of his sermons as read. The printed sermons of many distinguished preachers unveil no power to account for their popularity. Those who ascribe the charm of these fragmentary remains simply to beauty of style and the congeniality of their doctrinal teaching to the unrenewed heart, evince an incapacity to comprehend Robertson or grasp the secret of his intellectual power. No one cause will account for this popularity, which is the result of several distinct elements of interest combined.

He grappled manfully with some of the perplexing problems of theology which disturb the minds of men; hence to those who had felt these difficulties his attempted solutions, whether entirely satisfactory or not, would possess a special attraction. Much also was due to the fact that his inquiries led him in the direction in which a portion of the theological thought of Britain and America was already drifting. He had a rare capacity of sympathy with the most diverse feelings. It is a great point gained when we feel that a preacher or writer understands our doubts and can fully enter into our perplexities. His natural courage brought out in bold relief his independence as a thinker. He dared to utter whatever he believed to be true. He hurled stern words of rebuke against every form of oppression, and spoke tender words of sympathy with humanity in every condition of sorrow. His denunciations of all wrong-doing were fierce and blistering, something in which men of different creeds could unite and sympathize. But above all these is the glowing earnestness of his soul. His thoughts are on fire. His mind is a volcano, throwing out in liquid streams the mental ore that has been dissolved by its intense heat. Not the beauty of his style, though his language is often eminently felicitous and expressive; not the grandeur of his thoughts, though frequently truly sublime; not the keenness of his intellectual glance, which often, like sheet-lightning in the darkness, unveils a hidden world of thought; not the logical force of his arguments, in this they are often deficient; but above every other source of attractive interest we are disposed to place the fact that they are the utterances of one who has himself felt deeply, and struggled anxiously to solve the perplexing problems of being and truth. Every thought has been molten in the furnace of his own heart before it was coined into those burning words that quicken the pulses of the blood, and convey to the heart of the reader something of the emotional warmth in which they originated. He possessed that indefinable thing which we call genius; whose potency we feel but cannot describe. In the suggestive fragments he has left behind him it may be truly said,

> "Bright-eyed Fancy, hovering o'er,
> Scatters from her pictured urn
> Thoughts that breathe and words that burn."

We come now to a question of far higher import than the cause of Robertson's popularity, namely, wherein did he differ from the acknowledged tenets held by evangelical Protestants? And is he on these points sound and true, in harmony with "the Scriptures of truth"? No matter how brilliant his genius or how beautiful his speculations, if his doctrinal teaching is not founded upon truth it is unworthy of confidence, and only the more dangerous from its attractiveness. And no matter whether he is accounted orthodox or heterodox, as compared with sectarian and human standards, if his teaching is true it will live in spite of all opposition.

Robertson himself gives us a key to much of his teaching when he represents himself as seeking to discover "the soul of good in things evil," seeking to find deep and important truths hidden under the form of familiar and acknowledged errors. This is strikingly displayed in his treatment of Roman Catholic errors, for which he had generally some word of apology to offer. He saw in Mariolatry an attempt to realize the idea of a pure and perfect womanhood, by those who had not recognized that in Christ the highest virtues of the race, male and female, are embodied and illustrated; in the doctrine of purgatory he saw the expression of a hope that pain in the future world may be "remedial and not penal," at least "to those who are neither heavenly nor damnable"; in the apostolical succession he saw "not the power of God conveyed by physical contact, not a line of priests, but a succession of prophets, a broken and scattered one, but a real one." He thought "that ultra-Protestantism missed the truth contained in transubstantiation," namely, "that the sacrifice of Christ is repeated daily in the hearts of all faithful people, forever going on, but not in the sacrifice of the mass"—whatever that may mean. In absolution he discovers "the forgiveness of man as man, carrying with it an absolving power," "that the minister absolves as the representative of humanity"; as "a type and assurance of divine forgiveness."

Now it is doubtless the duty of all candid seekers after truth to practise to some extent this method. We should not give an unconditioned condemnation of a person, without examining all modifying circumstances that may lessen his culpability; nor of an opinion without inquiring what degree of truth may exist in union with the error it contains. But, when such search becomes the habit of the mind it has grave disadvantages. It tends to make us think lightly of error. There is no heresy but may contain some latent truth. But the danger is, that minds on the alert to discover whatever truth any wrong opinion contains, will forget the virulence of the falsehood in their satisfaction at discovering some element of truth. An error may be grave and fatal, and yet contain some portion of truth. What is false may be active, while the truth is latent and even unapprehended. The truth found in union with falsehood is often nothing more than the beverage in which the poison of error is dissolved. There is also a dangerous tendency in such minds to soften the evil of error, by certain fanciful discoveries of truth and goodness that will not bear close scrutiny. This defect is unmistakably illustrated in many of the expositions of doctrine given by Robertson, which are obscure and fanciful.

But it is not only to acknowledged errors that this method is applied. The tenets of Protestantism, as popularly understood, are all to him errors from which he extracts the truths they contain. Under this treatment the name of a doctrine may be retained, when it no longer represents the same truth, and is not used in its historic sense. Prayer, Regeneration, the vicarious Atonement of Christ, the Inspiration of the Scriptures, etc., may be spoken of with due frequency; but they must be very easily satisfied who take it for granted that these terms are used by him to represent the same ideas which they represent in the historic theology of the Church. We will briefly glance at his views on two or three points which illustrate this assertion.

The doctrine of baptismal regeneration Robertson firmly rejected. But he regards it as based upon the alleged truth that all men are by nature the children of God, and that baptism authoritatively declares and specially reveals this fact. Hence he confesses that practically there is little difference between himself and the Tractarians on this point. If his statements merely related to infants, they would be less exceptionable. But he has no idea of any such limitation. He distinctly rejects "that view which maintains that you are not God's child until evidence of a regenerate life is given, until signs of a converted soul are shown;" and boldly declares that human "nature became, viewed in Christ, a holy thing and divine;" that "the appearance of the Son of God is the sanctification of the human race." Is it possible that any one who knows and reveres the teaching of Divine truth can admit that a sinner, dead in trespasses and sins, is a child of God in any other sense than by creation? How can such an assumption be reconciled with St. Paul's statement, that Christians "were by nature the children of wrath, even as others?" Or with that of St. John: "as many as received him to them gave he power to become the sons of God?" Not the sinner in his sin, but "as many as are led by the Spirit of God, they are the sons of God." Nor is there any warrant for the assumption that baptism is the authorized revelation of our relation to God. How could it be such a revelation to an unconscious infant? Are not our relation to God and privileges through Christ revealed in the Word of God? Such fanciful theology may be acceptable to those who reject the inspiration of the Bible, but "we have a more sure word of prophecy, whereunto we do well that we take heed."

He regards the expectation that God will answer prayer by any direct interposition of His power, as contrary to the uniformity of the laws of nature, the facts of experience, and the character of God, and injurious in its influence on those who cherish it. In taking this view he assumes that mind and matter are governed by the same law; and that the power and freedom of God are limited by the forces of His material creation. Robertson is not the only theologian of our day who, while repudiating Pantheism, assumes positions that are essentially pantheistic.

He does not think that there is any authority, either in the Old or New Testament, for the Christian observance of the Sabbath; but that it rests solely on the necessity and advantages of observing the day as a day of rest, worship and recreation. He avows his acceptance of the doctrine of the Trinity, but the Deity of Christ is somewhat superfluous in his system of doctrine. He assigns no work to Christ as our Redeemer that requires or implies His Godhead.

Though he had an intense hatred of wrong-doing and admiration of goodness, yet he never seems to have grasped an adequate conception of the holiness and dignity of the divine law, and of the sinfulness of corrupt nature, preventing our access to God and requiring an atonement to vindicate the dignity and stability of the law and the holiness and mercy of the Lawgiver. He rejects that theory of the Atonement which represents Christ as suffering the penalty of sin and the wrath of God, and human guilt being cancelled in the ledger of heaven by His righteousness. But he does not indicate any acquaintance with that view of the Atonement which regards the sufferings of Christ as an equivalent for the penalty, the result, not the cause of divine mercy, whereby the outgoings of divine mercy are harmonized with the claims of divine justice, and the power of infinite love is unveiled, to subdue the sinful heart to penitence and obedience. He speaks of the vicarious sufferings of Christ, and of his reconciling man to God, but he gives no reason for the necessity of his suffering. In answer to the question, "If God is love why do we need a Mediator?" he replies, "I think the best answer is, I do not know." Now Robertson is daring enough in speculation when it suits him to be so; and the mediation of Christ is a great central truth which must have some discernible fitness, arising out of the character of God and the moral condition of men. And if so great a fact appears as a superfluity in his system of theology, it may justly create a doubt that his conception of man's relations to God is not in harmony with truth.

His conception of the results of the Atonement are equally hazy and unsatisfactory. He indeed represents Christ as reconciling man to God, man to man man to himself, and man to duty. But all this is accomplished by the influence of His holiness and self-denial operating upon our minds, and leading us to imitate His example. In Christ dying for all he finds no higher meaning than that "He was the victim of the sin of all," and that "His sacrifice represents the sacrifice of all." That is that he suffered from his contact with the universal wickedness of men, and that His suffering is the type of what we must suffer! He says, "The value of the death of Christ consisted in the surrender of His self-will. . . . the profound idea therefore contained in the death of Christ is the duty of self-surrender. . . . He [God] saw humanity subject to the law of self-sacrifice, in the light of that idea He beholds us as perfect, and is satisfied." Thus the great scriptural truth, that Christ died for our sins and that we have redemption through His blood, is dissolved into airy mist and supplanted by fanciful and baseless speculation, the meaning of which is very hazy.

Robertson also rejects the doctrine of a direct revelation from God of special truth to the minds of the writers of the Holy Scriptures. He says, in one of his letters, " The difference between Moses and Anaxagoras, the Epistles and the 'Excursion,' I believe is in degree. The Light or the Word which dwells in all men, dwells in loftier degree in some than in others. . . . I think this view of the matter is important, because in the other way some twenty or thirty men in the world's history have had a special communication, miraculous and from God. In this all have it, and, by devout and earnest cultivation of the mind and heart, may have it increased illimitably." In his sermon on "The Good Shepherd" he says, "There is a something in our souls of God, which corresponds with what is of God outside us and recognizes it by direct intuition : something in the true soul that corresponds with truth, and knows it to be truth." This view of Inspiration cuts away at a stroke "the promises of God," and deprives Bible teaching of any just claim to be called "the Word of God." "If any man," says Paul, "thinks himself to be a prophet or spiritual, let him acknowledge that the things which I write unto you are the commandments of the Lord."

We do not believe that we are left without any means of knowing truth from error, and right from wrong. But we believe in using all the faculties with which we are endowed, reason as well as intuition. We confess that some theologians have not duly recognized these capacities of the soul with which God has endowed us. But to assume that "nothing is more evident than truth," that the soul intuitively recognizes it and needs no evidence from the reason, and no authority of an objective revelation, is to contradict the whole moral history of our race, and to overlook the spiritual condition of men as portrayed in the Holy Scriptures and confirmed by history and observation. To speak as if the natural feelings and impulses of men are a safe law of life, is to forget that dark and evil passions have seized the helm of the soul and are steering it on toward destruction. It is misleading and fallacious to speak of the feelings of men enslaved by passion, prejudice, and ignorance as if they were the intuitions of a pure and elevated humanity. If men were perfectly holy their convictions respecting truth would, doubtless, be widely different. But of what practical value is this conclusion, so long as the supposition on which it rests is not true? If our belief in ordinary facts depends upon the authority of testimony, why may not our belief in the great doctrinal facts of the Gospel rest upon the authority of the testimony by which they are sustained? These theories may be true of the inhabitants of some other sphere but do not fit here. On the contrary, the authoritative revelation of His will, which God has given to be an objective law of life, is eminently adapted to the condition of beings liable to error, and "having the understanding darkened through the ignorance that is in them."

I cannot pursue this subject further. It has not been my purpose to offer a formal refutation of what I deem erroneous; but simply to point out what is objectionable in this teaching. What has been said may suffice to show the direction of F. W. Robertson's theological progress. There are doubtless many modifying considerations to be taken into account in judging of his theological position. It must be conceded that his sermons are not designed to form a system of theology, and were published without his consent or revision; that he sometimes expresses a familiar truth by language that gives it a new form; that his meaning is often obscure; that he is not always consistent with himself; that he was, to use his own graphic figure, like a pilot steering a zigzag course through dangerous rocks, and not to be judged by those who merely watch the vessel's course from the shore, and see not the rocks which he sees. But after making every concession that truth and fairness demand, it is beyond doubt that there is a broad and radical difference between many of his doctrinal views and the teaching of those who are generally regarded as the standard expounders of Protestant theology—not to say the plain teaching of the Scriptures.

Although an original and independent thinker, on important points, he is in substantial agreement with the Rationalists of the Anglican Church, as represented by the authors of "Essays and Reviews." He is, however, distinguished from them by his devout piety, and by being no mere iconoclast, breaking down without building up. He sought earnestly, and with great mental acuteness, to present positive views of the truth, which he believed to be more in harmony with the religious consciousness of the age. He was a Rationalist, with strong High-Church leanings, who never quite shook off the influence of his education among the despised "Evangelicals."

He always seems to assume that the teaching of the Anglican Church must be right, although he is compelled to put the most unnatural and fanciful construction on many of her tenets before he can adopt them as his own. He cherished a strong admiration for the character and writings of Channing, which was not without some influence on his ardent and susceptible mind. And in nearly every instance in which he forsakes the old landmarks of the theology of the Reformation, he drifts in the direction of the more evangelical Unitarians.

Some may deem our exceptions to his theology inconsistent with our expressed admiration of his character. We would cast no shade of doubt on the sincerity of his piety and the nobleness of his life. His life reflects honor on humanity. But we are not of those who allow their admiration for his excellences to hush all doubt regarding the soundness of his teaching. Let us not confound things that should be kept distinct. Are we to admit the Unitarianism of Channing, the election and reprobation of Calvin, the miraculous gifts of Irving, or the wild dreams of Swedenborg, because we admit that they were gifted and sincere men? Like Schleiermacher, Fichte and others, the piety of Robertson's heart seems to have shielded him from the logical consequences of the speculations of his brain. But this does not prove that his errors are harmless. The errors which are maintained by a writer are often more injurious in their influence on others than to himself. This was singularly so in the case of those German writers just mentioned. The philosophy that led others into Pantheism seemed to have had little practical influence upon themselves.

But the practical result of a general adoption of the views to which we have taken exception is scarcely doubtful. It may be that some who deny any scriptural authority for the Sabbath, and place its claims merely on the visible need and advantages of a day of rest, will from habits of piety continue to observe the day reverently; but will not the general promulgation of the doctrine that there is no divine authority for the Sabbath be adverse to its devout observance? Persons who have formed the habit of prayer may continue to observe this duty after they have ceased to believe in God as the answerer of prayer; but who will be induced to begin to pray that has no expectation of God answering his prayers? He who believes that all men are by nature children of God, and that this relation is declared and ratified by divine authority in baptism, can hardly feel that he needs to seek the regenerating grace of the Spirit, by which alone we can be born from above. It may be that some to whom the Bible has become precious, will continue to study and revere its teaching after they have adopted theories of inspiration which undermine its authority and rob it of its claims to our confidence; but what will be the effect of a general adoption of the belief that it merely contains the thoughts and feelings of good men, and in no proper sense the "Word of God," or a revelation of His will as the law of life? Such a belief cannot be entertained without a total revolution in our views of the relation of the Bible to the development of spiritual life.

We have spoken of Robertson as one of the signs of the times in theology, one of the indications of a tendency to greater latitude of speculation and a bolder and more relentless criticism; a tendency to give less weight to formal and rigid statements of doctrine and a higher place to the convictions of the conscience.* However it may be accounted for, this movement is sufficiently important to claim a candid, patient and intelligent investigation. There must be something in the present condition of theological science which has prepared the way for it. And as almost every heresy is an exaggerated truth that has not been duly recognized in the orthodox confessions of faith, there must be some element of truth in this movement to which it owes its strength. Is there nothing in dogmas based upon misconceptions of the

---

* This tendency has greatly increased and brought forth suggestive results since this essay was first published.

figurative and poetic language of Scripture, in stereotyped platitudes and half-truths being taken for the whole truth, thus teaching for doctrines of revelation the commandments and opinions of men, and in the want of a just recognition of the dignity of the individual conscience, from which this movement may be largely a reaction? One thing is certain: It cannot be put down merely by greater stringency in enforcing confessions of faith, or by dogmatic and intolerant denunciation. This would only strengthen it. Its errors must be calmly and fairly met by the force of truth. It will be well for the Church if she prove herself sufficiently liberal and discriminating to recognize whatever truth the movement may contain and the lessons it teaches, while holding fast with unabated confidence those great Scripture verities which have inspired her noblest achievements, and nerved the strength of the great "cloud of witnesses" who, " through faith and patience, inherit the promises."

II.

CHARLES SANGSTER, A CANADIAN POET OF THE LAST GENERATION.

THE poets of a country rarely receive from the general public the recognition they deserve. A due appreciation of their rank, for the most part comes late, and is confined to the few whom natural gifts and education have made susceptible to the influence of songs that "have power to quiet the restless pulse of care."

Too many fail to recognize the inspiring and refining power of poetry, and regard it as the idle dreamings of the imagination, when loosed from the control of the reason. And yet it would be easy to show how in most countries the national poets have strengthened the ties of patriotic unity, and stirred the hearts of the people to deeds of manly daring. The poetry of a country indicates, with tolerable accuracy, its place in the scale of intellectual culture and refinement.

But the true poet does much more than rouse patriotic sentiment by martial strains.

> "A priest, by Heaven ordained,
> The Poet-seer at Nature's altar stands
> To voice the reverent worship of his race;
> To coin in human language golden thoughts
> Bodied in matter's hieroglyphic forms,
> And sing the joys and griefs, the hopes and fears,
> Which thousands dumbly feel but cannot speak."

Whatever good things may be deservedly said of the younger Canadian poets, the people should not forget the pioneer bards of a past generation, who gave poetic utterance to the sentiment of a loyal patriotism, and made many Canadian scenes forever sacred by embalming them in descriptive verse. In this class Charles Sangster occupies a prominent place, and deserves the grateful remembrance of his countrymen.

As long ago as 1864, the writer of this article wrote and published in his "Selections from Canadian Poets," the following estimate of Mr. Sangster's poetry:

"We are disposed to think that any just estimate of Mr. Sangster's poetry will assign him the first place among Canadian poets. Others may have written as well and as sweetly on some themes as he could have done; but no one has contributed so largely to enrich Canadian poetry. No one has attempted so much. No one has displayed equal freshness and variety of imagery in the treatment of national themes. Indeed, in the variety of subjects selected from the scenery, seasons and past history of this country, and in the success and originality with which he has treated them, he has no competitor whatever. His genius is more truly Canadian than that of any other poet of distinction in this Province. Mr. Sangster, while cherishing a loyal attachment to the mother-land, gives Canada the chief place in his heart. Her mighty lakes and rivers—her forests and hills—her history, religion and laws—her homes and liberties—her brave sons and fair daughters—are all objects of his most ardent affection, graven alike upon the pages of his poetry and upon the tablets of his heart. The most prominent characteristics of his genius are, a wonderful fertility of thought, which enables him to pour forth images and forms of expression with lavish prodigality; an intense sympathy with nature in all her varied moods and forms; and that peculiar freshness and originality of language that is the sure distinction of those to whom belong 'the vision and the faculty divine.' Occasionally, too, we catch glimpses of a philosophic spirit, capable of grappling with the deep problems of the world of mind."

Since this was written a new generation of Canadian poets has arisen to enrich our native literature. They have given us many poems, marked by subtle thinking and rare descriptive power. They reveal the culture of our times in the deep inwoven harmonies of their verse. Yet they do not render this estimate obsolete or untrue. In some important respects Sangster is still the most representative of our Canadian bards. It is not merely that his themes are Canadian; he lived in an atmosphere of Canadian sentiment, and everything he wrote is permeated with the free spirit of the "grand old woods" and broad lakes of his country. Even the want of familiarity with the classical literature of the ancients, while it narrowed the range of his thoughts and deprived him of important advantages, made him more intensely the poet of the land and times in which his lot was cast. For this reason, I am sorry that his countrymen do not know more about the man and the productions of his pen.

The unfavorable circumstances in which his literary work was done may well evoke sympathy and admiration. It is not too much to say that among the many poets of Britain and America, who had through life to battle against unpropitious fortune, poverty and cold neglect, there is scarcely one who had a rougher or steeper path to climb, or who faced unfriendly fate with a braver heart than Charles Sangster.

Mr. Sangster was born at Kingston in 1822, and died at Ottawa in 1893. My personal acquaintance with him was very slight, but I had considerable correspondence with him on literary matters. In a letter to me, written in 1864, he gives the following facts respecting his early life:

"My father died at Penetanguishene in the service of the Navy Department, before I was two years of age. He had served a number of years in the navy as a joiner and ship-builder. He was the son of a U. E. Loyalist, one Charles Sangster, a sergeant in 2nd Battalion 60th Regiment, and was for some time in the 44th. He (my grandfather) served for a period of nearly thirty-two years, and was present under General Burgoyne through the American Revolution, where his Highland valor was no disgrace to his name, nor to the service to which he was attached.

"My grandfather Sangster was, I believe, from Leith, Scotland. My grandfather on my mother's side (Ross) was from Ross-shire. He settled at Prince Edward Island, and I think it was in 1802-3 that my parents left there, proceeding upward to Canada. So I suppose the Scotch will, with some show of justice, lay claim to me; although my grandmother on my father's side was Irish, and my grandmother on my mother's side was English almost, for the Munros, from which she sprang, could scarcely have been English. So you see I have the blood of the three kingdoms in me—the greater part being Scottish.

"My mother was left with a large family when my father died, I being the youngest. She was then at Kingston, where she resided ever since on the navy grounds, until last spring, when she went home. Having to work hard to maintain her family by the labor of her hands, it is not to be wondered at that I have not had the benefit of a classical education. But I remember having gone to several schoolmasters, who spoke most execrable English, and from whom I *didn't* learn to write my native tongue."

He was early forced to seek employment, in order to contribute something towards the support of the family. In the Ordnance Department at Kingston he spent nearly ten years, where he said he did clerk's work on laborer's pay. Becoming thoroughly tired of this, he finally left in disgust, and spent several years in different newspaper officers in various capacities. There is no doubt this work was somewhat more congenial, and was a valuable training. Had not his poetic instinct been irrepressible, it must have been utterly crushed by the weary grinding toil of so many years; but the spirit of poetry was a part of his being. In the later years of his life, he was a clerk in the Civil Service Department at Ottawa, a position which, while it kept him above actual want, was not adapted to develop a poet's gifts. The wonder is that he accomplished so much.

His first volume, "The St. Lawrence and the Saguenay, and Other Poems," was published in 1856.

Though not of uniform merit throughout, and sometimes bearing marks of want of time for elaboration, such as is necessary to a polished style, it was full of the fire and glowing imagination of the true poet, accompanied by a wealth of description, and a copious supply of fresh and picturesque language. The chief poem portrays an imaginary voyage of the poet, and some fair but shadowy companion, down the St. Lawrence and up the Saguenay. It consists mainly of descriptive references to places and scenes along the shores of these mighty rivers, and such poetic musings as these scenes, or the events of which they were the theatres, inspire. The Thousand Islands, Montreal, Quebec, and the bold scenery of the lone Saguenay, stir the soul of the patriotic bard, and call forth appropriate reflections. At intervals there is a burst of lyric melody from the voyageur, as if the measured movement of the more stately metre was too prosaic to fitly express the joyous admiration that thrilled him. Some of these are among his best lyrics. This poem contains one hundred and ten Spenserian stanzas. He informed me, several years before his death, that he had carefully re-written "The St. Lawrence and the Saguenay" for a new edition; but it has never been published.

In 1860, he published "Hesperus, and Other Poems," which showed a marked improvement in literary finish, and was very favorably noticed by English and United States' journals, as well as by the Canadian press. There is no labored effort nor straining after effect. His finest expressions are simple and spontaneous. So competent a critic as Oliver Wendell Holmes wrote: "His verse adds new interest to the woods and streams amidst which he sings, and embellishes the charms of the maidens he celebrates." Miss Ingelow wrote: "Mr. Sangster is a true poet, and his verses are all the more pleasant because he is never careless and never affected."

But, as in the case of nearly all poetic ventures in Canada, the popular demand for both volumes was discouragingly small; instead of being a source of profit, the proceeds of the sales did not pay the cost of publication. There must be a supply of "Hesperus" lying unsold somewhere to this day. This comparative neglect greatly disheartened Mr. Sangster. He felt that he deserved a more appreciative recognition than he received; and, beyond all question, he was justified in cherishing this conviction. As showing how small tokens of favor were gratefully appreciated, I may mention that he once wrote, saying, "Mr. Chauveau" (Superintendent of Education in Quebec) "wrote me that there was too much love in both my volumes to use them for school purposes. Not so bad for a Frenchman—but I fear he was right. He said, however, if I got up a selection from both, he would buy from fifty to one hundred copies every one or two years; and I thought this was a point gained, which might some day be put in practice."

Mr. Sangster was a keen critic of poetry, though he received courteously criticisms on his own work. A brother bard in his native city must have been personally, as well as poetically, disagreeable to him. He wrote, "Do you know anything of our Kingston Breakenridge, author of 'The Crusades and other Poems?' Since dead—both man and book—but I send you one of his poems, with my opinion of the book. I wish you had his volume, because we might differ in regard to his merits. He was a lawyer. He hadn't the soul of a poet, and was forever carping at every one who dared to write poetry. He could even sneer at Leigh Hunt." He afterward sent me Breakenridge's volume. It was no small jealousy that prompted him to write in this severe strain; for he spoke in warmest terms of several other Canadian poets. Of another Kingston bard, he said, "You should know Evan McColl, and if you ever make any stay in Kingston long enough, make his acquaintance by all means, and you will find him every inch a man."

As Sangster's volumes are in the hands of a very limited number of our people, I may be permitted to illustrate what I have said respecting the character of his genius, by a few brief citations from his poems. Occasionally there is an affluence of language, almost too splendid for the thought; but the expression of his thoughts is never tame or hackneyed. A striking poem in his first volume, entitled, "The Changes of a Night," opens with the imposing sentence—

> "Midnight had set her star-emblazoned seal
> Upon the slumbering world."

Then in a waking dream, memory portrays the beloved one of the vanished past. The old blissful hours are lived over again, surcharged with the old joy.

> "I saw her glide mysteriously past,
>   And felt the pressure of her heart-warmed hand;
>   The same rich music floated from her lips,
>   As when in happier days she sang to me
>   The tender ballads of a far-off land :
>   Her very breath was song, her words were odes
>   That set the pulses of the heart aglow
>   With a divine exuberance of love,
>   As pure as star-beams round the throne of night."

Here is a sonnet, entitled "Despondency"; though evidently the product of a morbid mental mood, it has a weird intensity of emotion in it, which makes it hard for one to read it without feeling something of the cowering dread it describes :

> "There is a sadness o'er my spirit stealing,
>   A flash of fire up-darting to my brain,
>   Sowing the seeds—and still the seeds concealing—
>   That are to ripen into future pain.
>   I feel the germ of madness in me springing,
>   Slowly, and certain, as the serpent's bound;
>   And my poor hopes, like dying tendrils clinging
>   To the green oak, tend surely to the ground;
>   And Reason's grasp grows feebler day by day,
>   As the slow poison up my nerves is creeping,
>   Ever and anon through my crushed heart leaping,
>   Like a swift panther darting on its prey;
>   And the bright taper Hope once fed within,
>   Hath waned and perished in the rueful din."

Mr. Sangster is at his best in his martial and patriotic pieces. His "Song for Canada," though perhaps too full of fight for members of peace societies, breathes simply the spirit of the man, when he sings in the first stanza,

> "Sons of the race whose sires
> Aroused the martial flame,
> That filled with smiles
> The triune isles,
> Through all their heights of fame!
> With hearts as brave as theirs,
> With hopes as strong and high,
> We'll ne'er disgrace
> The honoured race
> Whose deeds can never die.
> Let but the rash intruder dare
> To touch our darling strand,
> The martial fires
> That thrilled our sires
> Would flame throughout the land."

One of the most justly popular of our poet's pieces is "The Plains of Abraham," in which historic interest and the martial spirit are felicitously blended:

THE PLAINS OF ABRAHAM.

> I stood upon the Plain,
> That had trembled when the slain
> Hurled their proud, defiant curses at the battle-heated foe,
> When the steed dashed right and left,
> Through the bloody gaps he cleft,
> When the bridle rein was broken, and the rider was laid low.

What busy feet had trod
Upon the very sod
Where I marshalled the battalions of my fancy to my aid !
And I saw the combat dire,
Heard the quick, incessant fire,
And the cannon's echoes startling the reverberating glade.

I heard the chorus dire,
That jarred along the lyre
On which the hymn of battle hung like surgings of the wave,
When the storm, at blackest night,
Wakes the ocean in affright,
As it shouts its mighty pibroch o'er some shipwrecked vessel's grave.

I saw the broad claymore
Flash from its scabbard, o'er
The ranks that quailed and shuddered at the close and fierce attack ;
When Victory gave the word,
Then Scotland drew the sword,
And with arm that never faltered drove the brave defenders back.

I saw two great chiefs die,
Their last breaths like the sigh
Of the zephyr-sprite that wantons on the rosy lips of morn ;
No envy-poisoned darts,
No rancour in their hearts,
To unfit them for their triumph over death's impending scorn.

And as I thought and gazed,
   My soul, exultant, praised
The Power to which each mighty act and victory are due,
   For the saint-like peace that smiled
   Like a heaven-gifted child,
And for the air of quietude that steeped the distant view.

   Oh, rare, divinest life
   Of Peace, compared with Strife!
Yours is the truest splendor, and the most enduring fame;
   All the glory ever reaped
   Where the fiends of battle leaped,
Is harsh discord to the music of your under-toned acclaim.

Though he was not a religious poet in the sense of being a hymn-writer, there is always present, even when not expressed in words, the lofty faith in God of a reverent worshipper in Nature's vast temple. This spirit is seen in his fine prelude to "Hesperus:"

   "The stars are heaven's ministers,
      Right royally they teach
   God's glory and omnipotence
      In wondrous lowly speech.
   All eloquent with music as
      The tremblings of a lyre,
   To him that hath an ear to hear
      They speak in words of fire.

   "Not to learned sagas only
      Their whisperings come down;
   The monarch is not glorified
      Because he wears a crown.

> The humblest soldier in the camp
>   May win the smile of Mars,
> And 'tis the lowliest spirits hold
>   Communion with the stars.
>
> "Thoughts too refined for utterance,
>   Ethereal as the air,
> Crowd through the brain's dim labyrinths
>   And leave their impress there;
> As far along the gleaming void
>   Man's searching glances roll,
> Wonder usurps the throne of speech,
>   But vivifies the soul.
>
> "Oh, heaven-cradled mysteries,
>   What sacred paths ye've trod!
> Bright, jewelled scintillations
>   From the chariot wheels of God.
> When in the Spirit He rode forth
>   With vast creative aim,
> These were His footsteps left behind
>   To magnify His name."

In one letter, after referring tenderly to the death of his mother, he says: "There are gains for all our losses. And, while in this vein, I may say, referring to the closing paragraph of your letter, that, were it not for that 'other world,' 'the undiscovered country from whose bourn no traveller returns,' I should be the most miserable of mortals. Fame is dross to me. I write because I believe it to be a duty; and, succeed or fail, what little light I have shall not be hidden under a bushel. I have but one hope—one great hope—and it is great. You know it."

I cannot but think of Sangster's life as illustrating the spirit of John Milton, who in the days of his darkness said :

> " I argue not
> Against Heaven's hand nor will, nor bate a jot
> Of heart or hope ; but still bear up and steer
> Right onward."

I have a strong conviction that when the history of Canadian poets and poetry comes to be written, Charles Sangster will be awarded a more appreciative recognition than he received from the people of his own generation.

III.

JAMES ARMINIUS, THE GREAT DUTCH THEOLOGIAN.

IN the year 1560, in the pleasant little town of Oudewater, in the province of Utrecht, in Holland, a child was born whose future expositions of Scripture doctrine were destined to influence the currents of theological thought for all time; and who shall be held in honored remembrance as long as clear and powerful intellect, extensive and sound scholarship, consistent and devout piety, and rare force and massiveness of character, united in one person, can command the esteem and admiration of men. This was fourteen years after the immortal Luther had yielded up his brave spirit to God; forty-three years after he had begun the great Protestant Reformation, which broke asunder the fetters of centuries, and shed the light of divine truth upon thousands darkened and enslaved by ignorance and superstition; and four years before the death of the stern Reformer of Geneva, who has given his name to a severe but compact system of theology. Beyond all question, James Arminius was one of the world's truly great men—

> "One of the few, the immortal names,
> That were not born to die."

"He being dead yet speaketh." Like one of those tarnished paintings of the old masters, which, when the encrustations of time have been removed, shines forth with pristine beauty, the character and work of Arminius, after the lapse of three centuries, have risen out of the obscuring mists of theological prejudice and bitterness in fair and stately proportions, furnishing another remarkable example of men to whom after generations have awarded the just fame which was denied them by the narrow bigotry of their own times.

No subject has greater claims upon the studious attention of thoughtful minds, than the life-work and teaching of the men who have moulded the thought and action of the world. No desire to exalt piety by depreciating intellect should lead us to disparage the endowments, with which God has enriched those whose genius vindicates their right to kingship in the different provinces of the world of mind. Great men are God's precious gifts to a world that sadly needs them. Eminent theologians, philosophers and reformers, whose labors are in the sphere of mind and moral truth, are not less truly benefactors of the race than those whose inventions and discoveries have lightened labor and bestowed upon their fellow-men more palpable benefits. Great thinkers and workers in the sphere of political, social, and religious reform, are the leaders who through many a Red Sea of opposition and reproach have led the fainting and vacillating hosts of humanity into goodly possessions, which they could not have won without such leadership. They are discoverers, who find out truths long hidden from common sight; inventors who enrich us with new methods of work, more conducive to success; captains, who organize and lead men to victory.

As the best army requires a skilful general to direct its movements, so the moral and mental forces of the world need organizers and leaders, to render them powerful for good and permanent in their results. They lift up the standard of rebellion against mental serfdom, and teach men the value and dignity of freedom of thought. Such great souls deserve to be held in everlasting remembrance. For, as certainly as we owe political liberty to the heroic defenders of national independence, who shed their blood upon the battlefield resisting the tyranny of oppressors, we owe our intellectual and religious freedom to those who, in spite of danger and death, bravely uttered their unfaltering protest against the dominant errors and canonized fallacies of their times. Their noble deeds and words reflect light upon the path of life for those who come after them. Thinking over their inspiring thoughts, looking out upon the problems of being through their unscaled eyes, coming into sympathetic contact with their noble spirits, and feeling the power of the motives which impelled them onward in their high career, our narrow misconceptions are corrected, and we are lifted out of ourselves into a higher plane of being, than without their influence we could ever have attained. Without the leadership of Luther and Melancthon, the light of the Reformation might have been quenched in Germany, as it was in France. Without the organizing genius of John Wesley, Methodism in England might have been only a temporary revival, followed by a reaction, that would have overwhelmed with a tide of ungodliness the ground which had been for a time rescued from the surging sea of sin. But there is a right and a wrong use we may make of the great men of past times. It is right to honor their work, to avail ourselves of their studies and researches, to copy their spirit and practise the virtues that made their lives sublime. It is wrong to accept their decisions with unquestioning faith, or render them a slavish homage that tends to dwarf our intellectual manhood, and prevent needed reform and progress.

Though it is commonly known that the teaching of Methodist theology respecting Predestination, the Freedom of the Will and Universal Redemption, is in harmony with that of the great Dutch theologian, it is not so generally known that nearly all the doctrines which have special prominence in Wesleyan Theology were held by Arminius. In his "Declaration of Sentiments," as in most of his writings, he is defending himself against charges of false doctrine; his language is, therefore, guarded, as he desires to show that he is in harmony with the creed of the Reformed Churches of Holland, and to give his opponents no advantage against him. Yet he clearly states his belief that it is the privilege of believers to have the assurance of Adoption, "as well by the action of the Holy Spirit inwardly actuating the believer and by the fruits of faith, as from his own conscience and the testimony of God's Spirit witnessing together with his conscience." He was charged with holding that Christians may, by the grace of Christ, live without sin. His idea of Christian Perfection is substantially the same as Wesley's. He is more guarded against formally rejecting the certain Final Perseverance of believers. But he frankly confessed that the possibility of falling from a state of grace appeared to him to be taught in the Word of God; he stated that he had taught "it was possible for believers finally to decline and fall away from faith and salvation"; and his definition of what he means by the Perseverance of the Saints is in perfect agreement with the uniform teaching of the Methodist pulpit and the standard theologians of Methodism.

We deem it, therefore, not inappropriate, by a brief notice of the life and theological views of James Arminius, to introduce to the notice of Canadian Christians one who has so largely influenced theological thought, and whose godly life so beautifully illustrated the truths of his teaching. It is strange, while there have been so many able expounders and defenders of the sentiments of Arminius, that, until a comparatively recent date, his complete theological works were not published in English. In 1825, James Nichols, a practical English printer, thoroughly versed in the Calvinistic controversy of Holland, translated and published one volume of his writings. This was followed by a second in

1828, with a promise that the work would be completed by a third volume. In 1843 a life of Arminius, with copius extracts from his writings, was prepared by Dr. Bangs, whose name is so well known in Canada, and published by the Harpers of New York. In 1853, the Rev. W. R. Bagnall, of the Methodist Episcopal Church, having translated the third volume and revised the volumes translated by Nichols, published, in three large volumes, the complete works of Arminius, with a brief biography. We know not whether these volumes (to which we are mainly indebted in the preparation of this article) ever went through a second edition. Though not constituting a systematic treatise on divinity, they discuss all the leading questions of Christian Theology, and present a rich treasury of instructive expositions of the doctrinal teaching of Holy Scripture.

But although his noble character, his fruitful life and the rational and scriptural system of theology, which has become the special heritage of Methodists, invest his life with an interest that should ever be sufficient to preserve it from the dust and mildew of forgetfulness, it must be confessed that Arminius is little more than a name without a history or character, to the great majority of those who believe and maintain those views of divine truth of which he was the most eminent expounder. Several causes have tended to produce this state of things. He lived at a period comparatively distant from the living present, which mainly absorbs the thoughts of men ; and he lived in a generation removed out of the "fierce light" which beat upon the first leaders of the Reformation. He was a great thinker, rather than a great leader or organizer of institutions. He was a native of a "foreign country" and wrote not in our English tongue. His style also has too much of the scholastic method of that day to be popular with modern readers, although it is far more simple and perspicuous than that of most of his contemporaries. Above all, the hostility of the dominant Calvinistic party of his times misrepresented his opinions, and clouded his just fame by disparagement and slanderous allegations. And this wrong has been perpetuated from generation to generation, by theologians who take their views of Arminius from the false representations of his bitter opponents. Even to the present day he is represented as a Pelagian who denied the doctrines of grace ; and the term Arminianism is still used by some Calvinian writers as synonymous with the denial of Human Depravity and Justification by Faith. So far from this being true it is evident, from his early education and his desire to preserve harmony in the church of which he was a minister, that, like Wesley and the early Methodists, he sometimes "leaned too much towards Calvinism." Still further from the truth is it to speak of this eminent divine as if he were the author and inventor of the doctrines which he held. They are the doctrines of the Holy Scriptures and of the primitive Christian Church, in harmony with sound reason, though never before so fully expounded and defended as by Arminius in his refutation of the unscriptural fatalism of Calvin. Arminius cannot justly be held responsible for the erroneous views of many who have been called by his name in his own country. He is often incorrectly spoken of as the founder of a sect, which flourished for a while and then declined into insignificance. But he was not really the founder of any sect at all, though many of the Dutch Protestant churches accepted his doctrines, and were distinguished by his name, even when they had departed from his principles.

His influence on the world is that of the independent thinker and teacher of truth, and cannot be measured by those who are known by his name. So far from his influence having declined and passed away, his views are steadily gaining ground throughout the Christian world and never were so potent as to-day. Not only are his principles of theology accepted by the largest Protestant communion in the world, but those who are the natural heirs of the system he opposed are so gradually approaching his scheme of doctrine that were he to appear among us now, even modern Presbyterianism could scarcely whisper a breath of complaint against his religious opinions, that were deemed false and heretical by the disciples of Calvin and Beza, who in their intolerant zeal for their creed treated him so unjustly.

At the time of the birth of Arminius the mighty impulse which the Reformation had given to free religious enquiry had not yet died away. Religious questions were still the great questions of the day. Even national alliances and wars were governed more by religious than by purely political considerations.

The Protestant feeling and sturdy independence of the people of Holland were largely stimulated and developed by their heroic resistance to the oppressive and intolerant tyranny of papal Spain. Hence, the impulses acting on the society around him, as well as the severe struggle to which he was subjected by the death of his father while he was yet an infant, aided in bringing out his native force of intellect and character. His widowed mother, to whose sole care he with a brother and sister was left, was a woman of deep and earnest piety, whose spirit impressed itself upon the character of her gifted son. The family name was Herman, but following a common custom he adopted the name of Arminius, a celebrated leader of the Germans in the first century.

Though bereft of the instruction and support of his father, Providence opened up his way and raised him up friends. Theodore Emilius, though a Roman Catholic, had a great reputation for piety and erudition. He had learned enough of the Protestant faith to see and forsake some, at least, of the errors of Romanism. Prompted by the kindness of his heart and by admiration of the natural gifts of the poor fatherless boy, he took upon himself the expense of his education, and watched over his religious, as well as his literary training, with the greatest kindness and assiduity. Arminius made rapid progress in knowledge; and there is good ground to believe that in his boyhood he was truly converted to God; and thus laid the foundation of that life of devout piety, which was his highest distinction and the key to his character. Before he was fifteen his kind friend Emilius died, and left him once more to battle alone with unfriendly fortune. But God raised him up another friend. Snellius, a native of Oudewater, who was himself a man of learning, and who had been residing in Marpurg in Hessia to avoid the persecuting tyranny of the Spaniards, being on a visit to his native town was so favorably impressed with young Arminius, that he invited him to return with him and study at the University of Marpurg. The invitation was accepted thankfully. He went to Marpurg and entered the university, being then fifteen years of age. He had been there only a short time when he heard the terrible news that his native town had been sacked and burned by the Spanish army, which had butchered all the inhabitants. He at once started for Oudewater in deep anxiety about his friends; and probably with some faint hope that they had not all perished. But he found to his unspeakable grief that his mother, brother and sister, and all his relatives had been massacred by the barbarous Spaniards. With a crushed and bleeding heart he returned to Marpurg, walking all the way.

The same year the University of Leyden was founded by William I., Prince of Orange. As soon as Arminius knew that it was open for students he returned and entered it. Here he prosecuted his studies preparatory for the ministry for six years, with the greatest success. He left the university at the age of twenty-two, strongly recommended by the faculty to the authorities of the city of Amsterdam.

They assumed the expense of completing his education; and he, on his part, pledged himself to devote the remainder of his life after his ordination, to the service of the city. He went at once to study at Geneva, being attracted thither chiefly by the fame of Beza, who had succeeded Calvin as the chief expounder of the most extreme type of high Calvinism. Here his defence of the logic of Ramus against that of Aristotle gave such offence to some of the professors, that he was compelled to leave Geneva for the University of Basle, where he continued his studies for a year, giving at the same time lectures in theology. Such was the estimation in which he was held, that he was offered the degree of Doctor in Divinity by the University; but he modestly declined it on account of his youth. He returned to Geneva, prosecuted his studies in divinity there for three years longer, and secured the admiration and friendship of the learned Beza. During this period he offered no objection to the Calvinistic system of theology; but accepted it as the only scriptural and orthodox view of human redemption. But it gives weight to his later rejection of these tenets, that he must have been perfectly familiar with the strongest arguments of the master minds who maintained that system of doctrine now known as Calvinism. His rejection was the intelligent repudiation of the Calvinian system, by one who had thoroughly studied it.

After leaving Geneva, in company with several of his countrymen, he visited Italy and Rome. A strong motive in taking this journey was a desire to hear

Zabarella, then famous as a Professor of Philosophy in Padua. During this visit he had an opportunity of examining for himself the workings of Popery at its fountain head, and no doubt as in the case of Luther this confirmed and deepened his antagonism to the corruptions of Romanism. In 1588 he was licensed to preach, and after a short probation was ordained to the pastorate of the Dutch Church in Amsterdam; where for the next thirteen years he continued to exercise his ministry with eminent success and great popularity, especially with the laity.

In 1589 a circumstance occurred which deeply affected his whole future life. A pious Reformer, named Coornhert, had published an able pamphlet containing forcible arguments against Calvin's theory of Predestination, Justification, and the killing of heretics, being a report of a discussion between Coornhert and two Calvinist ministers of Delft. Some time after the Delft ministers published a reply; in which instead of defending the supralapsarian scheme of Calvin and Beza which Coornhert had assailed, they maintained the lower or sublapsarian view; and rejected the theory of Calvin. This kind of reply was unsatisfactory to the disciples of Calvin and Beza, who thought it should be answered. It is a tribute to the reputation of Arminius that, about the same time, he was urged by Professor Martin Lydius to defend his former teacher Beza; and requested by the ecclesiastical senate of Amsterdam to refute the alleged errors of Coornhert. He at once undertook the task. An examination of the controversy at first led him to favor the moderate, rather than the high Calvinistic view he had been requested to defend. But a full and impartial study of the Holy Scriptures, the early Christian Fathers, and the writings of the Protestant Reformers, led him to reject the Predestination of Calvin as contrary both to Scripture and reason. At first, for the sake of peace in the Church, he was very guarded in the expression of his views; but feeling that such a course was inconsistent with his duty as a professed teacher of religious truth, he began in his discourses, as occasion required, to expound the doctrines of the Holy Scriptures in accordance with his enlarged views of the Divine economy in the salvation of sinners. From this time forward, while his views gained many adherents among the thoughtful and unbiased, he was regarded by the ultra-Calvinists as a teacher of heresy, and bitterly opposed and traduced. Most distorted and unwarranted representations of his sentiments were circulated, with a view to injure his reputation and influence. But though feeling deeply the injustice of these assaults, he calmly prosecuted the work of his ministry, avoiding rather than courting controversy.

In 1590 he was married to Elizabeth Real, the daughter of a worthy judge and senator of Amsterdam. Their domestic life was eminently happy. They had seven sons and two daughters, who all died in early youth, except Lawrence, who became a merchant of Amsterdam, and Daniel, who was an eminent physician.

About the close of 1602, the death of Francis Junius, Professor of Divinity at Leyden, called the attention of the curators of the university to Arminius, as the most suitable person to fill the vacant position. This appointment was strenuously opposed by the authorities of Amsterdam, who wished to retain his services in their city, and also by Gomarus, the chief professor at Leyden, and many ultra-Calvinist ministers, who strongly disliked his anti-Calvinistic opinions. But after protracted negotiation, and a fuller explanation of his views by Arminius, the opposition was withdrawn and he was installed at Leyden as Professor of Divinity. On receiving the degree of Doctor in Divinity from the university, he delivered a masterly discourse on the Priesthood of Christ. The selection of a theme so close to the heart of the Gospel evinced the devout and practical bent of his mind; while the manner in which he expounded this great subject amply vindicated his fitness for the important position to which he had been appointed. On assuming the duties of his new position, he found that the students of theology were largely devoting themselves to the study of the knotty metaphysical speculations of the school-men, rather than to the great central verities of Christianity. He at once directed his efforts to correct this evil, and to bring them back to the direct and devout study of the Word of God, as the fountain of truth.

These efforts, and his known opposition to Calvinistic Predestination, provoked the hostility of Gomarus and those of similar views; and made Arminius the object of many bitter attacks and false accusations, which, however, he bore with great equanimity. He did not publicly defend himself till 1608, when he vindicated himself in a letter to Hypolytus; in an "Apology against thirty-one defamatory articles;" and by his noble and convincing "Declaration of Sentiments." The delivery of this elaborate and unanswerable discourse, before a full assembly of the States of Holland convened at the Hague, may be regarded as the culminating event of the public life of Arminius. The occasion was most imposing. He had for his auditors the chief men of his country, which then held a foremost place among the free and enlightened nations of the world. The questions discussed were the grandest and most important with which a human mind can grapple. The manner in which he expounded and defended his views of Divine truth was worthy of the occasion; and effectually confuted the accusations of his enemies, and forever vindicated the clearness of his intellect and the scriptural soundness of his theological opinions. Though touching briefly upon several points respecting which he had been misrepresented, he dwelt mainly on objections to the theory of Predestination maintained by Calvin and Beza. His refutation of this theory which had secured the allegiance of so many minds was complete and overwhelming. He did not confine himself to a few leading arguments. He swept the whole ground, piling up such an array of crushing objections that all which has been since written on that theme has been, of necessity, little more than an amplification of his arguments and objections. In addition to arguments against Calvinism based on its antagonism to the teaching of the Holy Scriptures, to the Gospel salvation, to the attributes of God, to the nature of man, to the nature of eternal life, to the nature of Divine grace, and to the nature and properties of sin, and objections based upon its being injurious to the glory of God, dishonorable to Christ, hurtful to the salvation of men, and in open hostility to the ministry of the Gospel, he shows conclusively that this doctrine was never admitted, decreed or approved in any Council, either general or particular, for the first six hundred years after Christ; that none of the Doctors or Fathers of the early Church who were regarded as standard authorities, held it; and that it did not agree with the Harmony of the Confessions that had been published at Geneva in the name of the Reformed Churches. It is difficult to see how any mind, open to the force of argument, could duly weigh the objections stated in this declaration of Arminius and yet hold the dogmas which he so trenchantly refuted.

Early in the following year a disease, brought on by unremitting labor and study, became extremely severe and prostrating. There can be no doubt that the pain inflicted by the bitter attacks of his intolerant persecutors greatly aggravated his disease and hastened his death. Though in great weakness and suffering, for some months he continued to lecture and perform other duties. On the 25th of July, 1609, he held a public disputation on " The vocation of men to salvation," which was his last public effort. He rapidly grew worse. Yet, in acute physical pain, he manifested no abatement of his usual cheerfulness and entire acquiescence with the will of God, till on the 19th of October at the age of forty-nine years, while surrounded by praying friends, his truth-loving and devout spirit escaped from the jarring strife of earth to the peace and harmony of heaven. In the words of one of his biographers: "He was distinguished among men for the virtue and amiability of his private, domestic and social character; among Christians, for his charity towards those who differed from him in opinion; among preachers, for his zeal, eloquence and success; and among divines, for his acute yet enlarged and comprehensive views of theology, his skill in argument and his candour and courtesy in controversy."

This high eulogy he justly merited. It is impossible to read his polemical discourses, which were often written in reply to what he considered to be severe and unjust attacks, without admiring the uniform Christian courtesy with which he discusses the questions at issue. No angry retorts or acrimonious expressions disfigure the calm and cogent presentation of his views. Not less admirable is the modesty with which he gives his judgment on the questions he discusses. Though he had during his whole life applied his great talents to the study of sacred subjects, he humbly speaks of himself as a learner willing to be taught, even by those against whom he contended in argument. While regarding with due respect the conclusions of the great men of other times, he called no man master. In his "Reasons for the Revision of the Dutch Confession and the Heidelberg Catechism," then the theological standards of the Protestant Churches of Holland, he pointed out clearly and wisely the danger of putting any human authority, however venerated, on a level with the Holy Scriptures.

In his views of the right of freedom of opinion, and in liberality towards those whom he thought in error, he was far in advance of his times; and even in our times but few have risen to his standard of charity and tolerance. Indeed, in his later years he was not so much of a mere advocate of a system of doctrine, as the champion of liberty of conscience and worship. Not that he was a latitudinarian in doctrine, or held his own convictions of truth lightly. But in the distinction which he recognized between truths that are essential to salvation and those that are not, he saw the ground for a comprehensive union between all who love our Lord Jesus Christ in sincerity, in spite of differences on non-essential points. This recognition of the right of freedom of conscience specially distinguished the Arminians of that day from the Calvinists. Shortly after the death of Arminius the States of Holland, acting by the advice of that noble Arminian statesman, John of Barneveldt, whose memory Motley the historian has so amply vindicated, issued an edict of full toleration to both parties, and prohibited the continuance of public controversy. The Calvinists refused to submit, and the strife became so furious that the Arminians found it necessary to protect themselves from personal violence by appointing a safeguard of militia-men. Like the Puritans of New England, the Calvinists of Holland, while protesting fiercely against the attempts of Rome to violate their consciences, had no idea of allowing liberty of conscience to those who did not accept their dogmas. Although it is our duty to "earnestly contend for the faith which was once delivered unto the saints" against all assailants, we should not too severely denounce those who persecuted the Arminians as heretics, unless we have learned to practise greater charity and toleration than they did towards those whose theological opinions differ from ours.

As we glance back along the ages, though saddened by the bigotry and bitterness with which those who named the name of Christ were sometimes arrayed against each other, we are cheered by catching glimpses of the many noble and heroic souls which rise above the darkness like divinely appointed sentinels, keeping watch over the welfare of a world that never knew their worth. To this immortal brotherhood belongs Arminius. The fogs of prejudice and intolerance, which so long obscured his just renown, are passing away forever.

> "Though round its base the rolling clouds are spread,
> Eternal sunshine settles on its head."

IV.

QUESTIONABLE TENDENCIES IN CURRENT THEOLOGICAL THOUGHT.

I. ALL who are interested in promoting the social and religious progress of the world should "discern the signs of the times." Teachers and leaders of men cannot fulfil their mission wisely and successfully, unless they have a knowledge of the forces that are operating around them, helping or hindering the work they are seeking to accomplish. There is no class to which this applies more pertinently than to ministers of the gospel. Doubtless it would be unwise for them to substitute the discussion of the heresies of the day for the verities of religion; but they should present these truths with an intelligent conception of the ideas and speculations that are occupying the minds of the people to whom they preach.

Nearly every age has been distinguished by some tidal wave of thought, or some tendency in a great degree peculiar to that time. Some of these were like the freshet from a summer shower, that soon passes away and leaves no permanent result; others, by virtue of the amount of truth they contained, left an enduring impression on the religious thought of generations following. The greatest danger to religion does not arise from opinions that are absolutely false; but from partial and exaggerated views which possess truth enough to make them plausible and popular; and yet are misleading half-truths, or speculations that are substituted for facts.

No one can deny that there are several features of the times in which we live, which are an undoubted improvement on the condition of things which existed in the Church of former ages. There is now more independent thought, greater regard for practical righteousness, and a profounder recognition of the rights of the common people. But there are, nevertheless, some questionable tendencies in current religious thought, against which it is necessary to guard.

II. Among the characteristic tendencies of the closing years of the nineteenth century may be named the undue exaltation of material good, as a remedy for human sin and sorrow. We are told that ministers spend their time preaching about sin and salvation to those whose chief need is better homes and better food and clothing. These ideas are frequently presented in a way which, without asserting it, implies that if people were only properly housed, clothed and fed, they would be moral and law-abiding without religion.

It would be folly to deny the evils of poverty, or the desirability of improving the condition of the poor and toiling classes. No one is worthy of the Christian name who does not evince practical sympathy with so laudable an object. What is to be deprecated is the substitution of material or social improvement for religion; as if a change of outward circumstances would prove a panacea for the ills and needs of humanity. The Master has taught us that the chief questions of life are not "What shall we eat? and what shall we drink? and wherewithal shall we be clothed?" It has been well said: "Our object is not a living, but a life." Man has moral and spiritual wants that only true religion can supply. He is guilty, and needs forgiveness; unholy, and needs to be renewed and sanctified; morally feeble, and needs strength to resist temptation and obey God, which only divine grace can impart. It is mockery to offer material things in answer to the anxious question: "What must I do to be saved?"

Among the censors of the Church and the pulpit there are many "blind leaders of the blind," who have never learned the great truth that "a man's life consisteth not in the abundance of the things which he possesseth." We have seen those who were amply supplied with all the good things of this life selfish, mean and wicked, proving that the possession of wealth does not bring depraved human nature into harmony with the divine will. It is equally true that many who have been sorely oppressed by poverty have lived brave, useful and unrepining lives, illustrating the truth of the apostle's declaration that God hath "chosen the poor of this world, rich in faith and heirs of the kingdom which he hath promised to them that love him." There is abundant evidence in the lives of Christians in all ages that a devout trust in God has shed light on many a dark lot, and sustained and comforted in circumstances of severe poverty and suffering.

III. There is a widespread tendency at the present time to speak in laudatory terms of the heathen religions, as if they were only a little inferior to Christianity, and therefore that the adherents of these systems cannot be in any great need of the gospel. This view was greatly strengthened by the homage rendered to the heathen religions at the Chicago Parliament of Religions; although the representatives of these systems had evidently borrowed what was best in their ideas from Christianity. We should not deny or disparage the truths found in heathen literature. No doubt there are many in heathen countries yearning for light and seeking after God. I fully believe that all that is good and true in human beliefs comes from God; and that "in every nation he that feareth Him and worketh righteousness is accepted with Him." It is unwise to dogmatize about the fate of the heathen. We may safely leave their future destiny in God's hands. "Shall not the Judge of all the earth do right?" But the practice of some Christian preachers and writers, who seem to think they evince their superior liberality and knowledge of advanced thought by exalting heathen systems, is neither in harmony with the Scripture estimate of heathenism, nor the undoubted facts which a close acquaintance with the actual moral and religious condition of the heathen world reveals. The Holy Scriptures never regard the

Christian religion as merely one of the great religions of the world. They recognize no fellowship with heathenism. They have no word but pity and condemnation for those who are in ignorance of the one living and true God. The apostles never discovered that the ignorance, false beliefs, and depraved moral condition of the heathen did not expose them to the danger of being lost, or did not create an obligation to bring them the good news of salvation through Christ. The great commission of the risen Saviour was not a mere arbitrary command to test the obedience of His apostles. He laid the obligation of preaching the gospel "to every creature" upon His Church, because the moral destitution of the world rendered this message of life necessary. The great apostle of the Gentiles had no sympathy whatever with modern Rationalist ideas about the sufficiency of the heathen religions. Speaking of the time before their conversion, he tells the Ephesian converts that "at that time ye were without Christ, being aliens from the commonwealth of Israel, and strangers from the covenants of promise, having no hope and without God in the world." It would be strange if such an estimate of their condition was not a powerful motive, impelling him to bring the message of life to those "who were dead in trespasses and sins."

One would need to go to the dark places of the earth in order to fully realize their great need. The missionaries in heathen lands, who have come into personal contact with the results of heathenism, bear uniform testimony that the state of the people in these lands strongly appeals to Christian sympathy. There may be found here and there some redeeming features, but the best pictures are dark enough. After years of missionary life, the missionaries know of no better way of rousing Christian interest in mission work than the simple recital of facts that show the spiritual need of the people, and the salutary changes that have been wrought by the gospel.

Whatever truths may be found in heathen literature, and however earnest souls in heathen lands may be seeking in darkness for the light of life, in no case has there been found a heathen religion that has vindicated its adaptation or power to supply the spiritual wants of its votaries. In most cases these so-called religions have dragged their adherents down to a lower level, and bound them in the slavery of misleading superstitions. The reformed Hindooism of the Indian Somajes is largely an attempt to pass off Christian ethics under Vedic names.

We need not wait to settle the differences of opinion about the destiny of the heathen before deciding that their condition lays weighty obligations on us to send them the gospel. They are ignorant of the true God and His revealed will. None of these systems give any definite answer to the deepest questions of the human heart. Is there a personal Creator who is interested in the children of men? What is the character of this great Being? What are His attitude and disposition toward His intelligent creatures. What are the duties He requires of them? How can they obtain deliverance from the burden of conscious guilt? Does the Creator hear and answer human prayer? When men die, does death end all? If there is a future life, what relation does the present life sustain to it? The devotees of systems that give no certain answer to these questions of profound and universal interest, are surely in a condition which makes it the duty of the Christian Church to send them the good news of life and salvation.

IV. Probably the most questionable characteristic of current theological thought is the prominence of opinions and theories which tend to substitute something else for the authority of the Bible. It is remarkable how many of the modern lines of thought converge toward the rejection of all external authority as a ground of belief, and the making of every man an oracle to himself.

There is a widespread disparagement of doctrinal creeds and beliefs; as if they were hindrances to right conduct, instead of being the roots from which right actions grow. This is not seen so much in direct denunciation of doctrines, as in the presentation of views of character and duty which assume that the belief of the doctrines of religion is a thing of very secondary importance. No doubt human creeds have been unduly revered, as if it were a virtue to profess an orthodox faith, whether it prompted to deeds of righteousness or not. The danger, however, at the present time is to go to the other extreme, and make light of religious beliefs. It is most unreasonable to maintain that it is important to have true views and beliefs about all temporal affairs; but that what we think and believe about spiritual and immortal interests is a matter of little or no consequence. There is reason to think that in some cases, at least, this disparagement of doctrine is the outcome of a desire to be free from the obligation to accept the teaching of the Bible. Disbelief or doubt of their truth must precede this antagonism to all formal statements of what is believed to be taught in the Scriptures. No one who believes the doctrines of the Bible to be true will deem the believing acceptance of these truths unimportant. It is true a mere profession of faith has no power to transform the character or control the life; but a living faith in the truths of religion has been the inspiration of the noblest lives. "As a man thinketh in his heart, so is he." Dr. John Watson's question, "Will the final assize be held on faith or character?" comes very near being a misleading quibble. It is freely admitted that the final assize will not be held on the faith professed in the day of judgment. The Scriptures clearly teach that the judgment will be on works and character; but assuredly not on works and character produced without faith; but on works which were fruits of faith.

V. The common practice of Rationalist critics to regard the Christian Scriptures simply as the literature of the Hebrew race, the product of a naturalistic evolution, has widely infected the theological thought of our day, within the Church as well as in the outside world. All duly attested facts, relating to the dates and authorship of the books of the Bible, we are bound to accept, whether they agree with our previous opinions or not. But the conclusions of critics who come to the Bible with a preconceived rejection of the supernatural interposition of God in human affairs, and who in their criticisms make everything bend to fit their theory, should be received with great caution, if not with actual distrust. It may be freely admitted that valuable light has been shed on many points by recent critical research; but the "results of criticism" are not all of equal value. They remind us of the ships of Tarshish, which brought not only "gold, silver and ivory," but also "apes and peacocks." The right of free discussion must be held sacred; but the right to reject what we consider is not sustained by adequate proof is equally sacred. Professor Sayce, the eminent oriental scholar and archæologist, says of the "advanced critics": "Baseless assumptions have been placed on a level with ascertained facts, hasty conclusions have been put forward as principles of science, and we have been called upon to accept the prepossessions and fancies of the individual critic as the revelation of a new gospel." And yet there is a surprising readiness to accept the conclusions of this school of critics as oracular deliverances, that it is an evidence of narrowness to question.

We are often told that the "higher criticism" only deals with literary matters, and does not affect the doctrines of the Bible. This is not correct. Much more than literary questions is involved. The truth and trustworthiness of the sacred writings are challenged and denied. If the method which some critics pursue, of setting aside as an interpolation any text that stands in the way of some preconceived view, be generally adopted, no one can tell how soon critical emergencies will arise, when passages which set forth precious vital doctrines shall be rejected by such criticism. We can hardly conceive of men who have accepted these low ideas of the inspiration and authority of the Scriptures engaging earnestly in evangelistic work, for which faith in veritable promises of God is an essential qualification. Those who deny that God interposed in human affairs in the past, are not likely to retain faith in Him as the answerer of prayer now.

The Rev. Lyman Abbott is a learned, able, and popular minister, who has largely adopted the conclusions of the German biblical critics. No one questions his sincerity or independence; but his work on "The Evolution of Christianity" and his other writings show that he has found it necessary to deny or remodel the doctrines of Christianity, in order to adjust them to his views of evolution. When the old words are retained, they are emptied of their historic meaning. After stating the doctrine as held in the Christian Church, he says: "The doctrine of the fall and of redemption, as thus stated, is inconsistent with the doctrine of evolution. It is impossible to reconcile the two." So, of course, the doctrine of the fall and redemption must go. Revelation, in the sense of truths made known to men by a personal

God, he also rejects. He says: "Revelation is the unveiling in human consciousness of that which God wrote in the human soul when he made it." There can be no difficulty in reconciling evolution, or anything else, with the Christian religion, if the reconciler is allowed to reject what cannot be reconciled, and to substitute for Christian doctrines some vague and spurious imitation of them which accords with his particular views. We may justly apply to Dr. Lyman Abbott what Mr. Gladstone said of Matthew Arnold: "He combined a fervent zeal for the Christian religion with a not less boldly avowed determination to transform it, beyond the possibility of recognition by friend or foe." Those who have been trained in the evangelical faith may retain much of their early beliefs, after accepting the advanced critical views; but will those, who from their youth have been brought up in the belief of negative views of the inspiration and authority of the Scriptures, be likely to hold fast those doctrines which are the foundation of experimental religion?

VI. There is a kind of teaching about the "living Christ" which, though appearing to honor Him and evince faith and piety, seems to make faith in the risen Saviour virtually independent of a belief of the statements in the Gospels concerning Him. The argument is that those who are saved and have communion with Christ have sufficient evidence to believe in Him as a living Saviour, whether the Gospel accounts be held to be true or not. It is freely admitted that the experience of salvation and communion with God supply to the believer the most satisfying evidence of the truth of Christianity. Every saved sinner has in his own experience proved the truth of promises of the word of God; but the experience of the blessings of salvation is ordinarily a result of the believing acceptance of the testimony of the evangelists concerning the life and character, the death and resurrection of Christ our Saviour. It is assuming a great deal more than is justifiable, when it is supposed that the Christian's faith and fellowship with Christ would continue the same, if the truths concerning Christ on which his faith rests were disproved or rejected. All we know of Christ we have learned from the New Testament. This is "a more sure word of prophecy" than an assumed ability to discriminate between the Persons of the Trinity with whom we have communion, which some pious mystics have claimed for themselves.

Another phase of this theory is that, because we have a living Saviour, we are not dependent on the Bible for our knowledge of divine truth. Hence, we need not go to the writings of prophets and apostles for such knowledge; but may go to the same source from which they received their revelations of truth. We are told that inspiration was not peculiar to the authors of Holy Scripture; that it is an abiding gift; that the Council of Nice had a right to claim that its deliverances were given by the Holy Ghost, as truly as the decrees of the apostles and elders recorded in the fifteenth chapter of the Acts.

Christian experience verifies the truths of the

Gospel; but it is not the medium by which we receive the knowledge of these truths. All Christians acknowledge that there are blessed promises of light and guidance for God's children in all circumstances; but the Spirit is not given to supersede the written word, or the exercise of our mental faculties. There is a clear distinction between the ordinary operations of the Spirit, whereby He enlightens and strengthens believers, and the inspiration by which holy men of old, who wrote the Scriptures, "spake from God, being moved by the Holy Ghost."

The Rev. Dr. Horton, in one of his Yale lectures on preaching, used these words: "Every living preacher must receive his message in a communication direct from God, and the constant purpose of his life must be to receive it uncorrupted, and to deliver it without addition or subtraction." If we understand this deliverance to mean what the words plainly express, Dr. Horton declares that the truths the living preacher utters in his sermons are a special revelation to him from God. This would lift him above the necessity of studying the Scriptures, or the book of nature, to learn the will of God. According to this, every "living preacher" is a walking oracle, with whom it would be utterly futile to reason or argue respecting his views; for he could silence every objection by the claim of a special revelation from heaven. Have we not here a form of priestly pretension that exceeds the claims of the Pope? No matter how sincere and pious those who propagate such views may be, they depreciate the authority of the Bible, and place themselves on the level of prophets and apostles. If the Christian preacher devoutly studies the Scriptures of truth, praying for divine light to enable him to understand the will of God, and faithfully delivers to the people the message of Bible truth which he has obtained as the result of such study, he may truly claim to have a message from God to the people, without laying claim to a special revelation.

VII. It is a significant fact that several of those writers who avow the purpose of exalting Christ as the supreme authority in religious truth, have deemed it justifiable to remand the authority of the apostles and prophets to an inferior plane. They speak as if only the very words of Christ, which constitute such a small part of the sacred writings, possessed divine authority. This is not in harmony with the testimony of the prophets in the Old Testament and the apostles in the New Testament, regarding the manner in which they received their revelations of the truth. The Lord Jesus, when about to leave His apostles, said unto them: "Howbeit when He the Spirit of truth is come, He shall guide you into all the truth." St. Paul, speaking of the gospel which he preached, said: "For I neither received it of man, neither was I taught it, but by the revelation of Jesus Christ." Yet, according to certain current ideas, we are to test the teachings of the apostles by their agreement with our understanding of the words of Christ, before we can be satisfied of their truth. No Christian will question the supremacy of Christ. The question is not, as Dr. John Watson ("Ian Maclaren") somewhat adroitly puts it, whether Paul was, "in the affair of teaching, not only the equal of Jesus but His superior" —" whether Paul claimed to be on the same level of authority with Jesus." No one, so far as we know, takes this position. This is not the necessary alternative of those who reject Dr. Watson's depreciation of Paul's authority as an inspired teacher of truth. The question is: Was Paul so divinely inspired that what he taught was according to the mind of Christ, and therefore truth worthy of our implicit confidence? We can answer this question with a decided affirmative, without any idea that we are setting the authority of Paul above that of Christ. When we accept the teaching of one of the Hebrew prophets as indubitable truth, divinely revealed, we are not placing the authority of the prophet above that of Him who chose him as the agent by which the truth should be made known. Paul's exaltation of Christ does not depreciate his own claim to be divinely inspired. It is not too much to say that some writers who profess to exalt the teachings of Christ as the extreme standard of truth, have interpreted His words so as to ascribe to Him the theories and beliefs which they have adopted as their creed. Then, anything in the writings of St. Paul or the other apostles that does not agree with these views is set aside under the pretext of honoring "the mind of the Master" above prophets and apostles.

It is a grave mistake to unduly magnify any one fact or truth, so as to overshadow or ignore other essential truths. The historic facts of our religion—the doctrines of the Christian faith—the moral precepts that are rules of conduct—the assurance of faith that is received in Christian experience—each is important in its own place. But no one of these should be substituted for another, or so exaggerated as to deny any other truth its legitimate place in the system of divinely revealed truths contained in the Holy Scriptures.

V.

THE TÜBINGEN SCHOOL OF CRITICISM.

HISTORY and biography are open books in which great lessons for our guidance are taught by living illustrations. The unity and essential sameness of human nature invest the history of human thought with perennial interest. For this reason there is a suggestive lesson for the present time in the rise and decline of the Tübingen school of criticism, with which the name of Ferdinand Christian Baur is inseparably connected as leader and founder. Though often referred to in theological discussion, yet, as the characteristics and outcome of that remarkable movement are not so well known by the present generation as they ought to be, a brief review of its rise and decline may not be without interest to many readers.

The University of Tübingen in Wurtemberg was founded before the Reformation, and after that event adhered to the Reformed faith. The attention attracted by the later "Tübingen School" has largely eclipsed the fact that, in the latter part of the last century, under the leadership of Gottlob Christian Storr and his associates, Tübingen was nearly as famous for its defence of the authority of the Scriptures and the historic docrines of Christianity, as it has been in this century for its negative criticism of the New Testament.

Ferdinand Christian Baur became a professor in Tübingen in 1826. In 1835, Strauss, who had formerly been a pupil of Baur, published his famous "Leben Jesu," in which he maintained the mythical theory of New Testament history. In the same year Baur published his work on the Pastoral Epistles, in which he advocated views of the New Testament which attracted wide attention, and which, when fully developed, made him famous as the founder of a new theological school. He does not seem to have been specially influenced by the theory of Strauss, as he had previously published and taught the main points of his own critical theory, which became the chief characteristic of the Tübingen school.

The distinguishing feature of this school of criticism was its denial of the genuineness of most of the New Testament writings, on the assumption that they were written at a later period than the age of the apostles, and of course by other authors than those to whom they are ascribed, for the purpose of setting forth theological views rendered necessary because of the conflicting beliefs which it was assumed had divided the Apostolic Church. In other words, it was held that Peter and the other original apostles and their disciples were simply Jews, who believed in Christ as the Messiah, yet retained all their Jewish narrowness; but that Paul and his followers divined the broader and truer conception of Christianity, as a universal religion which places believing Jews and Gentiles on the same level as children of God. So when this alleged division was healed during the second century, it was deemed desirable to prepare a Christian literature, and publish it as if it was written by the apostles and evangelists, in order to efface the evidence of the discreditable feud which had existed between the Pauline and Petrine parties in the early Church. It is with this theory, which became the corner-stone of the Tübingen school, rather than with any theological views, that we are concerned in these observations regarding Baur and his followers.

The way in which Baur came to adopt his peculiar view of the character and authorship of the books of the New Testament is not less suggestive than the theory itself. According to Professor Holtzmann, who is a Rationalist and a warm admirer of the "Meister," Baur was led to examine the epistles of St. Paul, "in the course of his study of Gnosticism, through his researches into the Homilies ascribed to the Roman Clement. In these Homilies he thought he discovered an abrupt opposition between Jewish and Pauline Christianity, in respect to which it was not easy to see how it could have been less in the preceding apostolic age. He investigated accordingly with more exactness the relation of St. Paul to the elder apostles, and found (as he thought) that the conception generally entertained of the apostolic age was a false one. It could in no way have been that golden age of undisturbed harmony which it was generally represented. On the contrary, the utterances of St. Paul himself afforded clear proof of deep oppositions and of vital struggles which that Apostle had to maintain with the Jewish-Christian party, and even with the older apostles."

The so-called "Clementine Homilies" mentioned by Holtzmann, Dr. Salmon, of Dublin University, describes as a kind of heretical Christian romance, written not earlier than the close of the second century. They are generally believed to have originated with a later sect of the Ebionites. They form a sort of controversial novel, in which St. Peter is represented as the Apostle of the Gentiles as well as of the Jews, and St. Paul is ignored, or even attacked under the disguise of Simon Magus. There is no satisfactory evidence as to who then held the sentiments these " Homilies " express, and consequently no ground to base important conclusions on their assumed widespread prevalence.

It is remarkable that it was not the study of the New Testament itself which suggested to Baur the idea of two conflicting theological schools among the apostles and their followers; but an anonymous heretical romance. It is not less strange that he should have concluded that the sectarian feeling displayed by this obscure Ebionite author, at the close of the second century, must have existed with equal intensity and affected the whole Church, during the lives of the apostles, one hundred and fifty years earlier. But the strangest thing of all, is that this supposed division of the Apostolic Church into opposing Pauline and Petrine theological factions, which in Baur's sense had no historic foundation, should be made the criterion by which to judge the authorship, date and genuineness of the books of the New Testament, and the justification for recasting the whole history of the early Church.

With this theory of the Pauline and Petrine cleavage in the Apostolic Church, Baur came to the examination of the books of the New Testament. He presents a striking example of the way in which a dominant preconceived idea can warp an acute thinker and vitiate his conclusions. As Principal Fairbairn forcibly remarks: "The conflict and reconciliation of the Petrine and Pauline tendencies accomplished most extraordinary feats in the realms of both apostolic and post-apostolic literature. Certain works were written to promote the first, certain others to promote the second, while a third class arose to reconcile the two." Every book in the New Testament was made to fit into some place in this theory of two theological factions in the Apostolic Church.

Baur found in the Epistle to the Romans and in that to the Galatians, as well as in the two Epistles to the Corinthians, some symptoms of division or jealousy which he regarded as proofs of his theory. Romans and Galatians vindicate justification by faith in Christ in opposition to salvation by the deeds of the law; and in the Epistles to the Corinthians there are references to local divisions. Some were of Paul, and some of Cephas, and some of Apollos. In the Epistle to the Galatians, Paul rebukes Peter's inconsistency. These things are taken as positive proof of the theory. So these four are taken to be genuine epistles of St. Paul. As there is no reference to the

Petrine and Pauline strife in the other nine epistles of St. Paul, this made it quite clear to him that they were not written by Paul, but by some late anonymous writer who ascribed them to the Apostle, with the pious design of covering over the old conflict and making future generations believe it never existed. The other books are dealt with in the same way. The Acts of the Apostles, with its account of the harmonious assembly at Jerusalem, which some call the First Council, and Peter's liberal preaching to the Gentile Cornelius and his family, stands right in the way of the Tübingen theory. It shows a condition of things in the Apostolic Church not at all in harmony with the fabricated history of Baur. So, in spite of the cogent historic and internal evidence of its genuineness, this book is cast out as a fiction founded on facts, written for the pious purpose of showing a unity in the Church that, according to this critical scheme, had never existed. The gospels and the other epistles are tried by the same test and share the same fate. As the Fourth Gospel is deemed the final and ideal document of the imaginary reconciliation, it receives special attention. It is regarded as an allegory written by some late author. The meaning of its events is expounded in a way that is as ingenious as it is fanciful and unnatural.

Not only was the New Testament discredited to adapt it to the Tübingen hypothesis, but other early Christian writings were judged by the same criterion and were similarly declared to be spurious. In all this criticism the historic evidence contained in the testimony of the Church was deemed of no weight when it contravened the positions adopted by Baur and his disciples. But it must be frankly acknowledged that extraordinary learning, ability and ingenuity were displayed in these efforts to make the books of the New Testament appear to furnish some confirmation of the views which Baur and his followers advocated.

The absence of a full history of what took place in the generation succeeding the apostles emboldened these critics to portray as historical a fanciful condition of things in harmony with their assumptions.

The methods and results of this new Tübingen school made a great impression. They created a new era in theology. They carried with them a great part of the German critical and theological world. Many of the older professors stood firm; but most of the younger professors in Tübingen and other universities hailed the critical theories of Baur as if they were the greatest discovery of modern religious thought. It was regarded by many as the highest point yet reached in the study of Christianity. In time a brilliant band of able and learned scholars rallied around the master, and expounded and defended his views in acute and learned works. Of these, Zeller, Schwegler, Ritschl, Köstlin and Hilgenfeld almost rivalled Baur himself in learning and critical acumen. There was a time in Germany when theologians who did not accept the methods and conclusions of the new school were objects of scornful pity. Principal Fairbairn, referring to these critical methods, says: "To be unwilling to use these, or to believe in the discoveries made by their light, was to be adjudged an ignoramus or a charlatan, or, worst of all, an apologist, which meant little else than a knave, or one whose only science was the misuse of knowledge." But all this has long been a thing of the past.

It cannot be denied that the interest aroused by the critical speculations of Baur and his school gave a new impulse to the study of the sacred writings of Christianity, and promoted a more thorough critical knowledge of the New Testament and the early history of the Christian Church. Neither is it questioned that there were Judaizing teachers in the early Church, and that many of the Jews who accepted Jesus as the Messiah never grasped the full spiritual breadth and freedom of the Christian religion. This naturally caused sectional feeling and greater or less disharmony. It is admitted that the early Church grew in the knowledge of Christ. On many points, as Prof. G. P. Fisher says, "the apostles were left to learn in the prosecution of their work, by the outward instruction of providential events and the inward illumination of the Spirit." But that there was such difference of belief and teaching between St. Paul and the other apostles as divided the Church into two opposing factions, and that most of the books of the New Testament were a late product of this conflict and its reconciliation, as the Tübingen school held, are assumptions that have no historic foundation. These speculative notions have been so amply and convincingly disproved, that even disciples of Baur have been forced to renounce the main position on which his conclusions about the different books were built. When the foundation was taken away the structures erected upon it could no longer stand.

It is not denied that important results of the critical study promoted by the Tübingen school remain, and that some who are in sympathy with rationalist speculations still cling to some of Baur's views; yet all who keep in touch with current Biblical thought must know that the main position on which his theory rested has completely broken down. The evidence in support of the early date and genuineness of the Fourth Gospel and the other books of the New Testament is much clearer and stronger now than it was before the rise of the Tübingen school.

Principal Fairbairn, though recognizing fully all that was good in this school, says: "The Tübingen criticism failed, almost as completely as the Rationalism and Mythicism it displaced, to bring us face to face with the historical realities, especially the living Person that had created Christianity. Even before Baur's death in 1860, his school had in reality ceased to be." It is not only orthodox theologians who testify to this failure. H. Schmidt says: "In his last years, Baur had a faithful disciple in Northern Germany in Holsten. Otherwise he stood almost alone." Holtzmann, an eminent Rationalist and warm admirer of Baur, rejects several of his conclusions respecting

New Testament books. Hilgenfeld, another disciple, does the some thing. Weizacker, Baur's successor at Tübingen, characterizes it as a prejudice to suppose that in the post-apostolic age there were only Paulinists and legalizing Christian Jews. He admits that the original apostles had never been specific opponents of Paul. He also admits the possibility of miracles as a necessary deduction from Theism, and the Johannine origin of the narrative parts of the Fourth Gospel. Ritschl, at one time an eminent member of this school, according to Holtzmann's account of his argument on the main theory, held that "there arose after the destruction of Jerusalem an Essene Jewish Christianity which Baur, in the course of his investigations into the Clementines, falsely conceived as a potent influence reaching back to the first apostolic Christianity." Even Rénan, in the last edition of his "Life of Jesus," argues forcibly against the idea that the narratives of St. John's Gospel are theological allegories, as the Tübingen critics had maintained. It would be easy to multiply similar testimonies on this point.

Scarcely any one will deny that Baur and his chief associates were eminently learned, gifted and sincere men. Why, then, it may be asked, did they prove to be unsafe and misleading teachers? A full answer to this question would require a statement of the facts and arguments by which their views were refuted. This is impracticable and unnecessary. I may, however, remark that the Epistles of St. Paul, which were appealed to as containing proofs of the views of the Tübingen school, supply no adequate evidence of what Baur assumed to be a historic fact; but they do contain conclusive proof that no such serious antagonism and division existed. The method of interpretation which the emergencies of their theory rendered necessary was fanciful, strained, and unreasonable. The whole movement was an extreme effort of acute and scholarly men, who had adopted naturalism as their creed, to eliminate supernatural divine interference from the origination of Christianity and its sacred writings. Hence, as in our own day, books that had been held to be divinely inspired were assigned to unknown authors, in a way that deprived them of their authority as standards of doctrine and duty. Had there not been a predisposition to deny all supernatural manifestations, it is hard to see how these efforts to account for the origin of Christianity by merely human means could have been so widely accepted. But people require but slight evidence to accept what they want to believe, or what supports an adopted theory.

There is in the rise and fall of this Tübingen school an important lesson against the study of the Bible with any preconceived theory; and also of the unwisdom of too ready a submission to the authority of critical experts who may have a great reputation for learning and ability. In an article on "The Historical Criticism of the New Testament," Principal Wace, of King's College, London, has some pertinent remarks on this point. After referring to the collapse of the Tübingen school, he says:

"In view of these results, it is surely time for Englishmen of all schools to ask themselves what is the value to be placed upon a kind of criticism which has proved itself, in so conspicuous an instance, to be capable of such portentous errors. People have talked for some time past about German scholarship and German criticism as if it had some of the attributes of Papal infallibility, or as though, at all events, it should be treated with general deference and submission; and it turns out that the hypothesis which in recent times laid the chief claim to this respect started from a blunder, proceeded by shutting its eyes to facts, and ended in conclusions now proved to be preposterous.

"Wellhausen and his followers are similarly endeavoring to explain the Old Testament as a natural human development by turning it topsy-turvy, and would make out that the Law of Moses is the product and not the starting-point of Jewish life and history; so that, as it has been concisely put, in place of the expression 'the Law and the Prophets,' we ought to speak of the 'Prophets and the Law.' This theory has been received with similar admiration in Germany to that which greeted the enterprise of Baur, and it has been echoed over here, in some quarters where more caution and sense of responsibility might have been expected, as the latest oracle of an infallible criticism. The history of the school of Baur will suggest to thoughtful minds the wisdom of exercising a good deal of patient reserve before allowing themselves to be much disturbed in either direction by this new hypothesis. It can hardly be supported with more brilliancy, or meet with more apparent success, than that of the Tübingen school; and it may meet the same fate."

VI.

CONFESSIONS AND RETRACTIONS OF AN EMINENT SCIENTIST.

ONE of the most interesting and instructive soul histories ever published is that of the late George John Romanes, the eminent expounder and defender of the theory of Darwinian evolution, as seen in his "Thoughts on Religion," which since his death has been edited and published by Canon Gore, the editor and one of the writers of "Lux Mundi." In some respects it is unique in religious literature. In this little volume Canon Gore places before us the means of tracing the process of thought by which an acute thinker and learned champion of anti-Christian agnosticism, without any external influences, came back to a position in which he admits the force and reasonableness of the arguments for Christianity being a divine religion.

As Moses was "learned in all the wisdom of the Egyptians," Romanes was certainly thoroughly learned in all the wisdom and philosophy of the school of skeptical science which rejects revealed religion. It is therefore of very great interest to study his criticisms of the fallacies that kept him so long in an attitude of antagonism to spiritual religion, and to note his reasons for accepting arguments in support of Christianity which at one time he deemed futile.

Not that those who are in sympathy with evangelical theology will accept all his later views and arguments; yet they are a most significant confession of the inadequacy of the beliefs he formerly avowed and defended with great positiveness as scientific conclusions. Others may have retraced their steps between as widely separated extremes; but I do not remember any case in which an author of equal learning, intellectual acuteness and authority as a master in skeptical science, has so frankly criticised and retracted his former views because he deemed them untenable.

The main interest of this book is found in the unfinished notes in which the writer gives his later religious conclusions. But there is also given a summary of one of his earlier works which shows his extreme anti-theistic views at that time, and two unpublished articles which give evidence of a transition back toward his early religious faith.

In 1873 George Romanes gained the Burney prize at Cambridge for an essay on "Christian Prayer Considered in relation to the Belief that the Almighty Governs the World by General Laws."

At this time he was only twenty-five years of age. In this essay, assuming, for the purpose of argument, the reality of a personal God and of the Christian Revelation, and also the belief that God governs the world by general laws, he admitted that for anything science had revealed answers to prayer might take place, even in the region of the physical, without any violation of the laws of nature. But not long after this he repudiated the position taken in this essay, because he rejected the truth of its assumption respecting the existence of a personal God.

In 1876 Mr. Romanes published anonymously, "A Candid Examination of Theism, by Physicus," in which strongly skeptical and anti-theistic opinions are positively asserted. As the latest notes, entitled "A Candid Examination of Religion," are written with direct reference to this work, a few quotations from the chapter in the earlier work in which his conclusions are summed up may be given, to show his extreme views at that time.

He says: "We first disposed of the conspicuously absurd supposition that the origin of things or the mystery of existence admits of being explained by the theory of Theism in any further degree than by the theory of atheism. Next it was shown that the argument, 'our hearts require a God' is invalid, seeing that such a subjective necessity, even if made out, could not be sufficient to prove—or even to render probable—an objective existence."

The argument "all known minds are caused by an unknown mind" he pronounced inadmissible. "The theory of the freedom of the will" he declares "at this stage of thought utterly untenable." He condemns John Stuart Mill's idea of design, but admits that creation may imply intelligence.

Again he says: "I regard it as of the utmost importance to have clearly shown that the advance of science has now entitled us to assert, without the least hesitation, that the hypothesis of mind in nature is as certainly superfluous to account for any of the phenomena of nature as the scientific doctrine of the persistence of force and the indestructibility of matter is certainly true." Nothing is more striking in the "Candid Examination of Theism" than the dogmatic positiveness with which he affirms his conclusions. He says: "I am quite unable to understand how any one at the present day, with the most moderate powers of abstract thinking, can possibly bring himself to believe the theory of free will" (p. 24). Again: "There can no longer be any more doubt that the existence of a God is wholly unnecessary to explain any of the phenomena of the universe, than there is doubt that if I leave go of my pen it will fall on the table" (p. 64).

It is unnecessary to quote further to show the extreme conclusions he adopted. But he did not adopt this bold unbelief without doing violence to the religious instincts of his nature. He says: "So far as the ruination of individual happiness is concerned, no one can have a more lively perception than myself of the possibly disastrous tendency of my work." He frankly declares: "I am not ashamed to confess that with this virtual negation of God the universe to me has lost its soul of loveliness."

In his Rede lecture of 1885 on "Mind and Motion" there are signs of a change of standpoint. He severely criticises the materialistic account of mind. He admits that the advance of natural science is steadily leading us to the conclusion that there is no motion without mind and no being without knowing. In the unpublished articles which Mr. Romanes left there are, in spite of their skepticisms, signs of drifting away from his extreme anti-theism.

In 1889, in a paper on "The Evidence of Design in Nature," he combats the argument of Mr. S. Alexander against design, viz., that "the fair order of Nature is only acquired by a wholesale waste and sacrifice." To this he replies: "But if the 'wholesale waste and sacrifice' as antecedent, leads to a 'fair order of Nature' as its consequent, how can it be said that the 'wholesale waste and sacrifice' has been a failure?" Canon Gore considers that the most anti-theistic feature in Romanes' essays is the stress laid in them on the evidence which Nature supplies, or is supposed to supply, antagonistic to belief in the goodness of God; but that as he came to apprehend more clearly the light which the character of God, as revealed in the Christian religion, casts upon the mystery of suffering, the force of pessimistic arguments was largely deprived of weight. It seems to us that the main difference between the anti-theistic and his later standpoint is that in the former he excludes every arbiter but the speculative reason; in the latter he recognizes spiritual insight rather than reason, as our chief guide. If in his anti-Christian period our author unduly exalted reason, by making it the only instrument by which we can obtain a knowledge of things relating to the spiritual world, it will seem to some that in his last notes he goes to the other extreme of unduly magnifying the faith-faculty, as if it were sufficient, without the aid of reason, to apprehend and attest religious truth. We cannot dispense with reason in the study of religion, because it is the faculty by which we estimate the value of evidence. But when he speaks of himself as a "pure agnostic" Romanes seems to mean simply that scientific reasoning cannot find adequate grounds for belief in God. He uses reason in a sense similar to that in which Kidd uses the term in his "Social Evolution." But this "pure agnostic" must recognize that God may have revealed Himself by other means than scientific ratiocination. He holds that God is not unknowable, but unknown by reason. The main purpose of these latest notes is to show that the appropriate organ for the ascertainment of moral truth is not reason, but faith and intuition. We cannot see why all the powers, intellectual and moral, should not be united in the discovery and attestation of religious truth. Some things in the "Thoughts" seem to imply this.

But we are not so much concerned with the mental processes by which Professor Romanes came to admit the force of the evidence for the truths of Christianity, as with the fallacies he rejected and the religious conclusions he finally accepted. Though he elevates the ordinary phenomena of nature into the sphere of the divine in a way that has a close affinity with modern Rationalism, yet he says: "Unitarianism is only an affair of the reason—a merely abstract theory of the mind, having nothing to do with the heart, or the real needs of mankind. It is only when it takes the New Testament, tears out a few of its leaves relating to the Divinity of Christ, and appropriates all the rest, that its system becomes in any degree possible as a basis of religion." He frankly admits that further thought has enabled him to discover serious errors, or rather oversights in the very foundation of his "Candid Examinations of Theism." "In that treatise," he says, "I have since come to see that I was wrong touching what I constituted the basal argument for my negative conclusion." In these later "Notes" he discusses "Causality," "Free Will," "Faith," "Regeneration," and other Christian truths, in a way that recognizes the positive strength of the historical and spiritual evidences of Christianity, and the reasonableness of personal conversion.

We have shown how dogmatically Professor Romanes repudiated the doctrine of human freedom, yet in these later notes, discussing the question whether our volitions are caused or not, he says: "If determined from without, is there any room for freedom, in the sense required for saving the doctrine of moral responsibility? I think the answer to this must be an unconditional negative." He who had formerly denied that theism cast any light on creation now admits that "if there be a personal God no reason can be assigned why He should not be immanent in nature, or why all causation should not be the immediate expression of His will, and that every available reason points to the inference that He probably is so." Though Professor Romanes seems to deny the distinction between the natural and the supernatural, and reaches his conclusions in a somewhat peculiar way, yet he comes in the end to substantially orthodox ground on most points. Some of his statements are eminently suggestive. A few examples will illustrate his latest position and views:

"The antecedent improbability against a miracle being wrought by a man without a moral object is apt to be confused with that of its being done by God with an adequate moral object."

"It is a further fact that only by means of this theory of probation is it possible to give any meaning to the world, that is any *raison d'être* of human existence."

"It is also a matter of fact that if Christianity is truthful in representing this world as a school of moral probation, we cannot conceive a system better adapted to this end than is the world, or a better schoolmaster than Christianity."

"Therefore it is as absurd to say that the religious consciousness of minds other than our own can be barred antecedently as evidence, as to say that testimony to the miraculous is similarly barred."

"I take it, then, as unquestionably true that this whole negative side of the subject proves a vacuum in the soul of man which nothing can fill save faith in God."

"All this may lead on to an argument from the adaptation of Christianity to human higher needs. All men must feel these needs more or less in proportion as their higher natures, moral and spiritual, are developed. Now, Christianity is the only religion which is adapted to meet them, and, according to those who are alone able to testify, does so most abundantly."

"It is the absence from the biography of Christ of any doctrines which the subsequent growth of human knowledge—whether in natural science, ethics, political economy, or elsewhere—has had to discount. This negative argument is really almost as strong as is the positive one from what Christ did teach."

"Only to a man wholly destitute of spiritual perception can it be that Christianity should fail to appear the greatest exhibition of the beautiful, the sublime, and of all else that appeals to our spiritual nature, which has ever been known upon our earth."

"The teleology of Revelation supplements that of Nature, and so to the spiritually minded man they logically and mutually corroborate one another."

These are remarkable utterances from one who had declared that theism no more accounted for the universe than atheism, and who boldly denied that the order of nature indicated an intelligent mind. The most significant thing in this remarkable religious experience is that the views set forth so positively as the unquestionable deductions of science, by one of the most eminent scientists of our day, should be formally repudiated by him as erroneous conclusions, based on false premises. The positiveness with which he asserted his early views strikingly illustrates his remark that scientific men as a class are quite as dogmatic as the straitest sect of theologians. There is a lesson here for those who assume so confidently that conclusions which claim to be the result of scientific methods of study are not to be questioned by ordinary mortals.

Canon Gore visited the dying professor, and in conversation learned more fully of his restoration to the religious faith that he had at one time so confidently rejected. The thoughts I have quoted from his last fragmentary writings prepare one to receive without surprise the statement of Canon Gore that the writer "returned before his death to that full deliberate communion with the Church of Jesus Christ which he had for so many years been conscientiously compelled to forego."

VII.

WHAT SHOULD MINISTERS PREACH?

WHAT are the proper themes for the Christian preacher? Most Christian people regard this as a settled question which requires no answer. Yet it has of late become a living question, owing to a widespread disposition to criticise and find fault with the current teaching of the pulpit. Both secular and religious periodicals have given considerable space to criticisms of the subjects of preaching, accompanied by intimations as to what should be the theme of the pulpit. The most prominent thought in most of these homilies is, that doctrines are of little value, and, therefore, preachers should make the social duties that arise out of the relations of life the chief feature of their message to the people. It is alleged that preachers preach metaphysical theology, and neglect to enforce the practical duties of life.

It may be freely admitted that ministers need to guard against taking too narrow a view of the scope of pulpit teaching. When St. Paul says to the Corinthians, "For I determined not to know anything among you, save Jesus Christ and Him crucified," he evidently did not mean literally that this should be his only theme; for in his epistles he discusses many other subjects relating to matters of belief and duty.

All questions of moral duty are fit topics for the pulpit. All themes, the discussion of which is in harmony with the mission of the Church in the world, are proper subjects for the Christian preacher. The range of topics presented in the Scriptures is by no means narrow; and a preacher may always feel that he is on safe ground when he is expounding and enforcing truths taught in the Bible. Should not a preacher condemn prevailing forms of injustice and sin? Certainly; and for so doing he has a fine example in the Hebrew prophets, those fearless preachers of righteousness who quailed not before the face of hostile kings. It will be admitted by everyone that ministers of the Gospel should earnestly co-operate in all movements designed to promote social reform and alleviate human suffering. The poor and suffering classes, from whatever cause their needs may have arisen, should never fail to have the earnest practical sympathy of the Christian preacher. In him they should always find a ready advocate and champion.

All this is freely avowed, without the least consciousness that in saying these things we are making any new departure from accepted Christian principles. But there is a good deal said and written in condemnation of present-day preaching that is neither sound nor fair. There are many instances of a zeal that is not according to knowledge. Some who assume to be critics and reformers display crudeness of thought and ignorance of the subject about which they write so flippantly. Signs are not wanting that many of these censors have a very limited acquaintance with the character of the preaching in our Protestant churches. At any rate, their characterization of the preaching in the churches will not be generally accepted as correct, by those who are in the best position to form an intelligent judgment in the case.

The disparagement of doctrinal preaching is one of the most characteristic features of current criticisms of the modern pulpit. If it be meant that human creeds are sometimes unduly exalted, and that dissertations on dogmas are not expedient in the pulpit, few will question this. But doctrines are the great truths of our religion, and therefore their exposition in the pulpit is eminently proper. The belief of these truths supplies the strongest motives to righteous living. A mere intellectual assent to a creed may be a fruitless thing; but a living faith in the truths of the Christian religion is not a vain thing. "As a man thinketh in his heart, so is he." No one who truly believes the great truths of divine Revelation relating to God and man, to duty and destiny, can deem it an unimportant thing whether they are faithfully set forth in the preaching of the pulpit or not. There is good reason to believe that many disparage the preaching of Christian doctrines because they do not believe them, or because they have some theories of their own which they desire to substitute for what they contemn.

It is sometimes urged as a complaint that ministers are no longer leaders of public and social movements in the localities in which they reside, as they were in former times. Nearly all the ministers with whom I am acquainted are men who are "ready to every good work." Yet, even if the allegation be in the main true, it is not a just reason for condemning ministers. If Christian laymen have been aroused to take a more active part in reformatory movements, we should rejoice that this is the case. But is not this, in most instances, a result of the very preaching that is condemned?

It is alleged that preachers should give special prominence to political economy, national politics, and all the social questions of the day. It may be freely conceded that the practical application of the moral teaching of Christianity to all the relations of life is an important part of the Christian preacher's duty. But everything that is true or right is not embraced in the Christian preacher's commission. The great mission of the preacher is to declare God's threatenings against impenitent sinners, to make known the way of salvation through Christ, and to teach the duty of righteousness and benevolence in every sphere of life. Rightly understood this embraces a wide range. The Gospel, fully preached, touches all phases of human life, and condemns every form of wrongdoing and injustice.

Some time ago the Rev. H. R. Haweis, of England, in an article in *The North American Review*, maintained that commerce, politics, newspapers, economics, novels, plays, current literature, theosophy, occultism, spiritualism, and Christian science are all legitimate subjects for the preacher. The man who can recommend such a conglomeration of themes cannot have scriptural ideas of the object of preaching, or of the value of the truths which constitute the burden of the Christian preacher's message. The regular selection of secular themes, instead of Scripture truths, as the subjects of sermons, can hardly be approved by any one who believes that the Church has a Gospel of salvation to preach to the world. It would be a deplorable thing if preachers, who stand as ambassadors for Christ, beseeching sinners to be reconciled to God, should take their ideas for preaching from men who have drifted away from the faith of the Gospel.

We have schools and colleges in which art, literature, physical science, astronomy, agriculture, metaphysics, biology, chemistry, and other branches of useful knowledge are taught. Will any one maintain that it is the business of the pulpit to undertake to teach such subjects, however important they may be, and to compete with the agencies now employed in the dissemination of general secular knowledge? For the preacher to drift away on any such line would be to disregard the direct command of Christ, and the teaching and practice of the apostles, and practically to confess either that the people did not need the Gospel message, or that it had no special adaptation to the wants and woes of a sinful world.

Doubtless, there is room for improvement in preaching, but I am not prepared to admit that in the preaching of to-day there is any general neglect to apply the principles of Christ's religion to the duties of common life. Even in the last century John Wesley, whose evangelistic work might be supposed to limit the range of his teaching, preached and published a series of discourses expounding and enforcing the practical duties enjoined in the Sermon on the Mount. The sermons that are published in volumes, as well as those printed in the newspapers, do not at all justify the charge that the preachers of to-day deal in discussions of abstract dogmas, and neglect to condemn the social and moral evils of the times. Ministers are not perfect, but they cannot be fairly charged with failing to apply Christ's teaching to the moral problems of modern life. All departments of knowledge may be used by the preacher to illustrate and enforce religious truth. At the same time it is certain that the discussion of political and economic questions in the pulpit, even when moral principles are involved, requires special wisdom and discretion.

The Chicago Advance not long ago had some judicious remarks on this subject, from which I select a few pertinent sentences:

"The fact cannot be concealed that the pulpit that undertakes to discuss questions of political economy puts itself into an extremely difficult and unsatisfactory position. . . It is a science, therefore, to be discussed either by specialists or by men of practical experience. The minister is neither; and when he undertakes to set forth his theories of the science, he is walking on thin ice. . . When he is preaching the Word of God, he is wielding a sword that is invincible."

VIII.

MORAL TEACHING OF THE OLD TESTAMENT.

IT has been shown in a previous essay that the trend of a good deal of the theological thought of our times is in the direction of depreciating the inspiration and authority of the Holy Scriptures. It was there shown that the current disparagement of doctrinal beliefs, even though based on Scripture, the exaltation of the heathen religions, the theory that the Scriptures are the product of natural evolution, and the claim that every believer may go to the living Christ and receive direct revelations of truth—are all exaggerations of truth which tend to substitute something else for the written Word, in a way that depreciates its value and authority.

It is easy to see how any one of these theories may be presented in a manner that would free those who accepted it from depending on the Bible as the only rule of faith and conduct. It is not going too far to say, that the chief danger to Christian faith in our day comes from the acceptance of theories which indirectly undermine the authority of the Bible.

Prominent among the signs of this tendency are the assaults on the moral teaching of the Old Testament. It is alleged that it presents unworthy conceptions of God, and that actions are recorded as being done with divine approval which indicate a low moral standard, inconsistent with the claim for the Book of being divinely inspired and containing a revelation from God. The alleged unscientific character of the Bible need not be referred to here, as this objection has often been answered.

The Christianity of the New Testament is so largely built upon the Old Testament, and the divine authority of the latter is so fully recognized by our Lord and the inspired writers of the New Testament, that it cannot be thrown overboard as if it was a weight that it was desirable to cast off, and to cut loose from which would be an advantage to Christianity. This is a grave error; the two Testaments must stand or fall together.

A suggestive controversy on this subject took place not long ago in the *North American Review*. That able writer, Prof. Goldwin Smith, who in late years has done much more to give public expression to skeptical objections than to strengthen faith or help the benighted into the light, published an article in which he characterized the Old Testament as "Christianity's Millstone." In this article he furbished up those objections to the Old Testament which have been regarded as the special stock-in-trade of skeptics and infidels, and presented them with unsparing vigor and fulness of arraignment.

A reply to this article was published in the same periodical by Dr. G. C. Workman. The main line of this reply was to the effect that Dr. Smith's objections only applied to certain views of the Bible, but were without force against "scholars" who accept the results of scientific Biblical criticism. Dr. Smith admitted the main contention in this reply. He intimated that it was not against those who hold Dr. Workman's Rationalist views of Bible inspiration that his objections were directed, but against those who hold the belief of the orthodox Churches.

I have no intention of here entering into a discussion of the points raised in this controversy. This would involve an examination of the whole question of inspiration. I may say, however, that the theory of plenary verbal inspiration, which assumes every word in the Bible, in historic chronicles as well as in prophecy, to be dictated by the Holy Spirit, is open to serious objections. It is not affirmed in the Scriptures; it is inconsistent with the use made of historic documents, and with the varying accounts of the same events and the different styles of the sacred writers. This view, which is not now widely held, gives undue force to objections that are based on some special incidents recorded in Scripture, which are deemed unworthy or immoral. But of this theory, even so sound a critic as Principal Cave says: "Whatever be the popular conception of inspiration, it would be difficult to find adherents of this mechanical theory among theological writers of to-day." From this it may be seen that such objections as those referred to are mainly based on assumptions as to what Christians believe about the Bible, which few theologians will accept or defend.

On the other hand, the theory which regards the

Old Testament as the product of evolution, and the inspiration of prophets and apostles as similar to the afflatus of the poet, meets skeptical objections against the divine inspiration of the Old Testament, by surrendering those characteristics which constitute the ground of its claim to inspiration in the scriptural and historic sense. If we lower the Bible to the level of the sacred books of heathenism, only claiming for it some degree of superiority, and magnify the human element in Scripture and minify or ignore the divine and supernatural, in order to evade the force of skeptical objections against the inspiration of the Old Testament, we pay a great price for an empty victory. Such a victory is defeat; for it gives up the very claim against which the heaviest artillery of the enemy has been directed, viz., the divine authority of the teaching of the Bible. Suppose it was contended that a certain Christian man cannot be the good man he is commonly believed to be, because of conduct inconsistent with his reputed character. Would it "vindicate" him and meet the objection to assert that his questionable conduct was not inconsistent with his real character, but only with the character ascribed to him? Yet this is virtually what is done with the Bible, by those writers who adopt a low view of the inspiration of the Scriptures, as a reply to the objections of unbelievers, who say that the contents of the Bible are inconsistent with the sacred character claimed for it by Christians.

The question, whether the Old Testament teaching

is immoral or not, should be decided apart from all theories of inspiration. If its religious precepts were shown to be immoral, this would be a legitimate argument against the divine inspiration of such teaching. But some things being in the Bible, which do not comport with a modern unbeliever's ideas of what it should contain, is not a proof that its standard of right and duty is immoral and false. The alleged immoral teaching must be first fairly proved before it can be used as an argument against the divine inspiration of the Book.

It is worthy of being noted, however, that the objections to the morality of the Old Testament are mainly based on incidents in the narrative portions of Scripture, which were either reproductions of previous records, or statements of things apparently within the personal knowledge of the writers. No theologian maintains that these chronicles were special revelations from heaven. We believe these historical writers were truthful and trustworthy; but even if any of these records contained a mistake or error on any point, this would certainly not disprove the inspiration of the prophets, who proclaimed great religious truths and predicted coming events which only God could have revealed to them.

We are not shut up to the acceptance of either the Rationalist or the verbal theory of inspiration. It is better to come to the study of the Bible without any preconceived theory, and to form our judgment of it from the character of its contents and the testimony of the prophets and apostles as to the way in which they received their revelations of truth. An eminent Biblical scholar, who has written with learning and rare discrimination of the inspiration of the Old Testament, says: "The prophets represented themselves as peculiarly the confidants, and therefore the messengers of Deity; and our entire examination of their position has strengthened our convictions of the truthfulness of these speakers for God." Every unbiased student of the Hebrew prophecies will be led to a similar conclusion.

The methods by which some writers have tried to show that the moral teaching of the Old Testament is "crude and low" cannot be commended for their fairness. To select as proofs of this charge exceptional events, like those of Jael and Sisera, Samuel and Agag, and the slaughter of the Canaanites, and to pass over the moral and religious teaching of "the Law and the Prophets," is certainly not the way to get a true idea of the ethical standard of the Hebrew Scriptures. It is freely admitted that there are incidents in the Old Testament which indicate a lower moral standard than that of the New Testament or the present time. But though we do not regard the Scriptures as a product of evolution, we admit that, as time went on, the Old Testament itself shows a development of doctrine and moral teaching. The fuller revelation of God's will shed clearer light on the duties of life. It is not generally deemed just to judge the acts of even good men by the standards of a time of greater light than that in which they lived.

We would not accept the deeds of wickedness, which

take place in Christian countries, as an evidence that the moral standard of the New Testament was "low and crude." The conduct of people generally falls below their standard of right. Why should a different rule be applied to the people of Israel? Our Lord, though He appeals to the authority of these Scriptures, intimates that some, at least, of these laws were given by Moses, in consideration of the special moral condition of the people for whom they were intended.

Those who uphold the moral teaching of the Old Testament are not disposed to imitate the practice of the "higher critics," and declare that every passage which does not agree with their views is an interpolation. But we do say, when we have the mind of God revealed in clear statements of human duty, we cannot easily be justified in so interpreting the Scriptures as to ascribe to Him an approval of deeds which His own laws and precepts positively forbid, even though some things in these ancient writings may be hard to explain. These moral precepts and truths are so numerous and explicit, that we are not left to exceptional and ambiguous incidents to know what the God of Israel approved, or to judge of the standard of morals among the Hebrew people.

We can best judge of the moral ideas of a people by their conceptions of God and duty. Tried by this standard the ethics of the Hebrew people were far from being low and crude. First of all, there should be a just recognition of the high ethical code embodied in the Ten Commandments. Even critics, who dislocate the Pentateuch into conflicting fragments, admit the early date of the "ten words." Here the worship of the one living and true God is enjoined; idolatry and irreverence are forbidden; the observance of a day of sacred rest, and obedience to parents, are commanded; murder, dishonesty, adultery and falsehood are solemnly forbidden; and even selfish, covetous desires are branded with divine condemnation. No one can truthfully say, that a people recognizing their obligation to observe such a moral code had a low ethical standard.

Men's conceptions of God indicate the character of their morality and religion. We know that ancient nations whose claims to culture and intelligence were not small, represented their deities as revelling in the same guilty vices as their worshippers. But what is the character of the God of the Old Testament? "A God of truth and without iniquity, just and right is He." (Deut. xxxii. 4.) "I am the Almighty God, walk before Me and be thou perfect." (Gen. xvii. 1.) It is admitted that the imperfection of language may have sometimes caused the ascription of human feelings to God. But in the eagerness of some to represent the God of Israel as a cruel tyrant, the glorious representations of His mercy and goodness, contained in the Hebrew Scriptures, are thrust out of sight. To Moses He revealed Himself as "the Lord God, merciful and gracious, long-suffering and abundant in goodness and truth." (Ex. xxxiv. 6.) The fatherhood of God was not, as some say, unknown till revealed by Christ. These Hebrew saints rejoiced to know that, "like as a father pitieth his children, so the Lord pitieth them that fear Him." (Psalm ciii. 13.) They knew that "the Lord is nigh unto them that are of a broken heart; and saveth such as be of a contrite spirit." (Psalm xxxiv. 18.) One of the early writing prophets says: "Who is a God like unto Thee, that pardoneth iniquity, and passeth by the transgression of the remnant of his heritage? He retaineth not His anger forever, because He delighteth in mercy." (Micah vii. 18.)

The Old Testament ideas of the duty of men to each other are worthy of their divine source. The same prophet just quoted gives this comprehensive summary of duty: "What doth the Lord require of thee, but to do justly and to love mercy, and to walk humbly with thy God?" (Micah vi. 8.) To the question: "Who shall ascend into the hill of the Lord, and who shall stand in His holy place?" the answer is: "He that hath clean hands and a pure heart, who hath not lifted up his soul unto vanity, nor sworn deceitfully." (Psalm xxiv. 16.) The Hebrew prophets faithfully condemned all forms of wrong-doing, because it was a settled principle of their faith, that "the face of the Lord is against them that do evil." (Psalm xxxiv. 16.) They denounced all unrighteousness with such searching power, that there is no form of wickedness in the earth to-day which does not come under their righteous denunciations.

We fully recognize the "grace and truth" that came by Jesus Christ. It is not, however, necessary to disparage the Old Testament, in order to honor the greater light of the dispensation of the Spirit. The

Old Testament representations of the majesty and goodness of God—its denunciations of all oppression and injustice—its rich treasures of godly experience—its lofty conception of personal righteousness—its sympathy with the poor and down-trodden—its prophetic revelations of great truths—and its inspiring predictions of the world's Redeemer, disprove, as with a voice from heaven, the unjust allegation that the moral teaching of the Old Testament is "low and crude."

IX.

THE LAST OF THE GREAT PROPHETS.

THE HEBREW PROPHETS.

THE prophets of Israel belong to all time. They speak to all human hearts. They constitute a grand succession of faithful witnesses for the one living and true God. Their prophecies illuminate the times in which they were spoken, and lift them out of the shadows of obscurity into a clear and permanent historic light. The mists of uncertainty cover the religious history of the centuries that follow the close of Old Testament prophecy.

A combination of unique considerations invests with undying interest the study of their character, their mission and their oracles. They were the unquailing preachers of truth and righteousness, in times of the greatest moral degeneracy. They were the chosen messengers of Jehovah, by whom He made known His will. They proclaimed the coming judgments of God against the nations that rejected His claims. "They cheered and animated the people of Israel in times of deepest depression, by inspiring predictions of a coming reign of righteousness, when a Redeemer should arise to turn away ungodliness from Jacob. They rose so high above the priests in character and influence, that those minor orbs are largely lost to sight in the blaze of their superior brightness. In the Jewish theocracy they were the lights and touchstones of the national conscience, blending earnest calls to repentance and obedience with wonderful predictions of coming events that were to affect the destiny of nations."* Why do we study their writings? Because they contain the great ethical and religious principles that are the foundations of faith and duty for all generations, and reveal Him before whose eye the future was an open book. The Christian Church, St. Paul declares, is "built upon the foundation of the apostles and prophets, Christ Jesus Himself being the chief corner-stone." Throughout the New Testament it is constantly assumed that the teaching of the prophets was supernaturally revealed and possessed divine authority.

Modern Critical Study of the Prophets.

A new and intense interest in these prophetic writings has been evoked in recent times, by the extent to which they have become subjects of close and learned critical study. If the large cairns of stones piled over the bones of those who fell on famous battlefields show where the fight raged most fiercely, and what points were deemed most important, the numerous volumes and articles in periodicals, discussing the prophets of Israel, bear testimony to the interest with which the learned world regards these ancient oracles. The indirect

*Jesus, the Messiah.

and incidental references to contemporary events, or the silence respecting such events—the style and mental idiosyncrasies of the writers—linguistic peculiarities which are thought to be characteristic of the language at some stage in its history—the way in which the ideas harmonize with the supposed condition of religious progress at certain times—the disentombed records of a forgotten civilization—all have been keenly questioned to give evidence respecting the dates, the authorship, and the purpose of these records of writers, who claim to speak as revealers of God's will to His ancient people.

It would be beyond the range of these introductory remarks to state what we deem the outcome of these microscopic, analytic criticisms of the Old Testament. But a brief reference to these results may be permitted.

It may be freely conceded that this critical study of the times and occasions of the prophecies, and of the condition of the people to whom they were originally addressed, has invested them with a far greater living interest than they have when read as isolated statements. To take an illustration from the New Testament. The tender sympathy which breathes through St. Paul's epistle to the Philippians is far better understood, when the epistle is read in the light of the peculiar circumstances of suffering and deliverance, under which that Church was founded by Paul and Silas. But this personal element does not lessen the truth and value of the teaching, which do not depend upon the local associations. But just because the occasion of a prophecy or psalm enhances its interest, many invent imaginary settings that have no historic foundation. Against this we must carefully guard. It is also safe to believe that the keen and exhaustive criticism to which these books have been subjected, though for a time it may disturb the faith of many, will ultimately tend to promote a more unfaltering confidence in revealed truths that have been tested by the severest scrutiny.

But though frankly recognizing the advantages accruing from modern critical study, it must be admitted that many conclusions have been set forth as the results of scientific methods of research, which do not appear to rest on anything more solid than conjecture; and which, to say the least, it is very difficult to harmonize with the scriptural and historic conception of the prophets, which regards them as holy men, who "spake from God, being moved by the Holy Ghost." It is important to remember that these conclusions are, for the most part, not new facts discovered by modern research, but inferences drawn, by a freer style of speculative criticism, from facts that have been long familiar to all intelligent students of the Bible.

Two Current Views of Prophecy.

Speaking broadly, there are two current views of Hebrew prophecy, which are dividing theologians into opposing camps. One view is that these prophetic oracles were special and extraordinary revelations of God's will and purposes, made known by Him to those whom He had chosen to be prophets. The other view is that these prophecies were the outcome of the evolution of Hebrew religious thought and life, produced under the ordinary operations of the Spirit on the minds of gifted and pious men. Those who hold the first named position maintain that the predictions of the prophets evince superhuman knowledge, such as none but God could reveal. Those who take the second view either eliminate prediction, or reduce it to a vanishing point. Archdeacon Farrar may fitly represent this school. He says: "And though the wisdom which can see the future in the germs of the present is so naturally an endowment of the illuminated soul, that definite prediction—almost always of events already on the horizon—is not excluded from the sphere of the prophet's work," etc.* That is, after trying to show that the prophet is simply a preacher, he admits that the prophet is not excluded from inferring near future events from the present state of things; because this is the natural endowment of all illuminated souls. That the prophets were preachers of righteousness, which has always been fully held in the Church, is in no way inconsistent with their being chosen of God to reveal the future doom of nations and the coming of the Messiah. Prediction and fulfilment are a divine method of religious teaching, by which God made known His character; as He says: "I am God, and there is none like me, declaring

* The Minor Prophets, p. 4.

the end from the beginning, and from ancient times the things that are not yet done." (Isa. xlvi. 9, 10.)

It may be admitted that some whose theories appear to ignore the supernatural, concede in words a divine inspiration, for which their system has logically no place.

The Appeal Should be to the Bible.

In deciding between these two views of prophecy, it is neither improper nor unscientific to go to the Bible itself for an answer. What have the prophets to say on this point? There can scarcely be any question that the testimony of the sacred writers, as to the way in which they received what they gave forth in prophecy, strongly supports the historic view. Professor Sanday, of Oxford, himself a liberal critic, on this point says: "The central phenomenon of the Old Testament is prophecy. The leading prophets all tell us under what circumstances they came to assume their office, and how they came to regard themselves as exponents of the Divine will. . . . The process is always extremely different from what it would be, if the prophet arrived at his insight into spiritual things by the tentative efforts of his own genius. There is something sharp and sudden about it. He can lay his finger, so to speak, upon the moment when it came. And it always comes in the form of an overwhelming force from without, against which he struggles but in vain."[*]

An appeal to the sacred Scriptures themselves

---

[*] The Oracles of God, p. 53.

amply confirms these statements. We have the full account of the call of Moses to the prophet's office, and of his efforts to escape from the responsibility it imposed upon him. The prophet Isaiah describes the sublime circumstances connected with his call to the prophet's work. Jeremiah tells with equal explicitness how he was inducted into his prophetic ministry, and how God's words were given him to speak. Ezekiel records the time and place when he received his commission as a watchman, to whom God said: "Hear the word at my mouth and give them warning from me." St. Paul similarly declares of the Gospel which he preached, "I neither received it of man, neither was I taught it, but by the revelation of Jesus Christ."

This testimony is clear and explicit. I confess I am disposed to distrust any theory which assumes that the critics know better than the prophets themselves the character of the revelations contained in their prophecies. If we reject the conception which the prophets cherished of their office and of the manner in which God made known His will to them, and substitute in its place some theory of evolutional development, their testimony is discredited; their oracles are no longer to us divinely-revealed messages; their writings are simply regarded as literary remains, which we accept or reject as they agree or disagree with modern theories.

Professor Marcus Dods, who is distinguished alike for his liberal views and his Biblical scholarship, says: "What we mean by revelation is, that certain men come to have thoughts about God and divine things, not only new in the world and more significant than other men have had, but also such as they themselves could not have conceived or arrived at without the extraordinary aid and suggestion of God Himself. Even when the thoughts may seem to grow up in their mind as other thoughts do, they are not their own thoughts, but God's. Though the revelation is made within the prophet's mind, and by a process which he may not always be able to distinguish from his ordinary habit of thinking, the matter conveyed to his mind is as truly a revelation from God as if it were uttered by a voice from heaven, or written with a supernatural finger. This is what is essential in revelation, that it be God's utterance to us—God not waiting for men to find Him out, but Himself coming and giving us sure knowledge of Himself."*

Principal Cave, of England, says: "The prophet, then—according to the Old Testament view of his function—interpreted to man revelations he personally received from God. Prophecy was not divination, but revelation. Soothsaying rested upon human presentiment; prophecy followed upon Divine inspiration. The prophet was conscious of being an organ of Divine communications. The words he spake he knew to be Divine words. In a word, prophecy was revelation, Divine knowledge divinely imparted. At least, such is the conception everywhere current in the Old Testament."†

* The Post-Exilian Prophets, p. 19.
† Inspiration of the Old Testament, p. 382.

I am free to admit that the question whether the prophets were chosen messengers of God, through whom He made a revelation of His will and purposes in the sense in which they themselves evidently believed, is of much greater importance than whether everything in the narratives copied from ancient documents is infallibly inerrant. It is not wise to indulge in speculations as to the mode in which the prophets received their revelations, or to adopt theories of inspiration not based on the Scripture records. On these points, we can know nothing but what we learn from the sacred writers themselves. They plainly declared that the religious truths they taught, and the events they foretold, were especially revealed; and therefore they were not a natural evolution of the religious thought of the nation. If we reject their testimony on this point as untrue, we cannot trust it in regard to other things.

The Author and Time of this Prophecy.

Nothing is known of the personal history of Malachi. He was too intensely occupied with his "burden" to Israel to leave any record of his parentage, time, or birthplace. Like the Baptist whom he foretold, he was the "voice of one crying in the wilderness, make straight the way of the Lord." From the fact that the name means "my angel" or messenger, and that it is repeated in this book, it has been questioned whether Malachi is a proper name. This has mainly arisen from the fact that in the Septuagint it is translated in the first verse, "his messenger," although the name Malachi appears as the title of the book. The most competent scholars hold that Malachi is a proper name. As the names of most of the prophets have significant meanings, there is no sufficient reason why the meaning of the word Malachi should be taken as evidence that it was not the prophet's proper name. In this prophet we have a striking illustration of the way in which the godly zeal and faithful testimony of a brave spirit survive in perennial freshness and power, when everything relating to his personal career has been forgotten for ages.

Respecting the time and circumstances in which Malachi exercised his ministry, the internal evidence is very strong. It is almost universally admitted that he was the last of the great Hebrew prophets. Some of the radical critics, with whom late dates for psalms and prophecies have become a mania, are disposed to place Joel still later; but a numerous array of eminent German and English scholars consider the grounds for this conclusion very slight.

The reference to the temple service shows that Malachi lived some time after Zechariah and Haggai; and the sins he rebukes, and the condition of the people to whom he speaks, furnish strong evidence that he was a contemporary of Nehemiah. Malachi says: "Ye have corrupted the covenant of Levi, saith the Lord of Hosts." Nehemiah complains in similar words: "They have defiled the priesthood and the covenant of the priesthood and of the Levites." Nehemiah earnestly labored to reform what he called "the great evil" of marrying strange wives. In Malachi, Jehovah denounces those who had "dealt treacherously against the wives of their youth," and of their covenant, and "married the daughters of a strange god." In Malachi the people are exhorted to "bring all the tithes into the storehouse." In Nehemiah's reformation the people bring "the tithe of the corn and the new wine and the oil unto the treasuries." In Malachi, God says: "Ye are gone away from mine ordinances and have not kept them." Nehemiah asks: "Why is the house of God forsaken?" Malachi speaks to a poverty-stricken and destitute people. Soon after this the people came to Nehemiah, saying: "We have mortgaged our lands, vineyards and houses, that we might buy corn, because of the dearth." No other undated writing in the Old Testament furnishes such strong proof of the time of its production.

It is the general opinion that these prophecies were delivered during the absence of Nehemiah, after his first governorship in Jerusalem. There is the strongest probability that as Haggai and Zechariah co-operated with Zerubbabel in his work, Malachi co-operated with Nehemiah; and that he represents the inner and spiritual side of the reformation, which was achieved under this godly and patriotic governor, after his second return to Jerusalem. Every genuine reformation has its root in a change wrought in the hearts and lives of the people, rather than in any external exercise of legislative or political authority.

The circumstances of the people to whom Malachi

delivered his message give special point to its rebukes and warnings. When the foundation of the second temple was laid, some "wept with a loud voice, and many shouted aloud for joy." When it was finished, we are told, that they "kept the dedication of this house of God with joy." Ezra re-established the ancient worship, and later Nehemiah built the wall and administered the government for twelve years. After this Nehemiah returned to the Court of Persia, and Ezra disappears from the scene. Then came a sad decline that crushed the hopes that had been kindled by the restoration from the exile. Eliashib, the High Priest, who was not in sympathy with the reforms of Ezra and Nehemiah, appears to have become the chief director of affairs, and great religious degeneracy followed. A spurious liberality, partly caused by contact with Babylonian ideas, became the chief characteristic of the time. The influx of the heathen population was encouraged. Mixed marriages with the heathen women were allowed. Divorces for the purpose became common. As the Levites were the chief opposers of this wickedness, their tithes were withheld, so that they were compelled to engage in secular labor. The Sabbath was desecrated. Idolatrous worship, if not actually practised, was not regarded with disfavor. Canon Rawlinson thus portrays the condition of things at this juncture: "Meanwhile they allowed the house of God to be 'forsaken,' the choral service to be discontinued, the treasuries to become empty, and the once crowded courts to remain without ministers or worshippers." This was the condition of faithless recreancy and wickedness, against which the last of the great prophets of Israel exercised his faithful and fearless ministry.

"The burden of the word of the Lord to Israel by Malachi" is in a most emphatic sense "preaching for the times." The sins of priests and people are portrayed and condemned. God's displeasure, and the consequences of their sins, in preventing blessings and bringing judgment and punishment upon them, are scathingly proclaimed. The transgressors are urged to repentance and obedience by dark threatenings, and by glowing promises of blessing which are conditional upon their turning from their evil ways. The prophecy closes with a prophetic announcement of the forerunner of the day of the Lord. We can only briefly notice some of the more salient points in this pointed and practical message to an erring and backslidden people.

The Sins of Priests and People.

The most prominent characteristic of this period, and that with which the warnings and expostulations of the prophet are most largely occupied, is the neglect of the law of Moses, and the imperfect and formal performance of such services as they still rendered. Where sacrifices and offerings were not entirely withheld, they selfishly offered the blind, the lame and the sick, what is called by the prophet a "polluted" offering.

One of the difficulties of this prophecy, which is

apt to perplex a thoughtful reader, arises out of these references to offerings. The prominence given to the payment of tithes and the observance of the Levitical law, as conditions of receiving the Divine favor, seems to be inconsistent with the essential importance of the moral and spiritual elements in religion, which is so fully recognized by the earlier prophets and also in this prophecy.

But it is not the formal outward acts, but the spiritual principles and faith that they represent and express, which give these duties their value and significance. An external act considered in itself may have no special import, and yet may be related to vital results. The lowering of a flag on a vessel is a mere mechanical act; but it may mean defeat and enslavement. The due payment of the offerings enjoined in the law may seem a small thing; but the testimony borne for God and righteousness by maintaining His worship and service is not an insignificant thing. When God says, "bring ye all the tithes into the storehouse," we are not to regard this merely as a command to pay the priests' portion of the corn and oil, but a demand for the living faith and loving obedience of the heart. Christ condemned the Pharisees who paid tithe of mint and anise and cummin, but "omitted the weightier matters of the law, judgment, mercy and faith," thereby teaching us that the law was something far deeper and broader than a code of outward observances. St. Paul, the great vindicator of justification by faith, says: "Wherefore the law is holy, and the commandment holy, and just and good." (Rom. vii. 12.)

We have seen in the books of Ezra and Nehemiah that one of the most glaring sins of priests and people was the putting away of their lawful Jewish wives, and the marrying of heathen women. This evil, which overwhelmed Ezra with piercing sorrow, calls forth some of the severest condemnation in this prophecy. The reference to this great wrong is one of the most striking passages in this book:

"Yet ye say, Wherefore? Because the Lord has been witness between thee and the wife of thy youth, against whom thou hast dealt treacherously, though she is thy companion and the wife of thy covenant. And did he not make one? Yet had he the residue of the spirit. And wherefore one? That he might seek a godly seed. Therefore take heed to your spirit, and let none deal treacherously against the wife of his youth. For the Lord, the God of Israel, saith that he hateth putting away" (ch. ii. 14, 15, 16).

The reasons for this condemnation are evident. It was a union with idolaters, that would hardly fail, as in Solomon's case, to turn away their hearts from the God of their fathers. Such marriages were also a treacherous violation of a solemn covenant, and a cruel abandonment of those to whom they owed faithful love. It is clearly intimated that it was contrary to the Divine purpose in the institution of marriage. He made one, because He sought a godly seed. There is something very graphic and suggestive in the thought that the altar of the Lord was covered "with tears, with weeping and crying out, insomuch that He regarded not the offering any more." The idea is that the altar was covered with the tears of the women who had been basely cast off; and therefore the prayers of the transgressor were disregarded; "because the Lord of the altar has been witness of the unfaithfulness consummated by divorce, of which they have been guilty towards the wives to whom they were bound by the tender recollections of youthful love, by the intimate companionship of married life, and by the solemn covenant which united them to each other" (Perowne). The thoughts here respecting the sacredness of marriage and the wickedness of divorce are almost identical with the words of our Lord on this subject, in reply to the Pharisees. (Matt xix. 9.) By Malachi, Jehovah declares that He hates divorce. We have no reason to believe that it is more pleasing in His sight now.

Because the priests, the religious teachers and guides of the people, were also guilty of this faithless ingratitude and disobedience, made it the more heinous and inexcusable in God's sight. Those who stood as watchmen and shepherds of the people, not only neglected their duty, but went with the multitude to do evil; therefore, their prayers were not accepted, and the threatening is pronounced, that if they do not hearken to the divine commandment to reform, He would curse their blessings. It is suggestive that in the prophetic announcements of the great reforms to be wrought by the manifestation of the Angel of the Covenant, it is said: "He shall purify the sons of Levi, and purge them as gold and silver; and they shall offer unto the Lord offerings in righteousness"—indicating that judgment would begin at the house of God.

This is not the only place in which the priests are blamed for the sins of the people. Jeremiah represents God as saying: "My people hath been lost sheep; their shepherds have caused them to go astray." In all periods of the history of the Church, unfaithfulness in doctrine and life, on the part of the ministry, has been accompanied by a low religious condition of the people.

The Character of True Ministers Described.

In striking contrast to the faithless and corrupt priests who had polluted the sacrificial service, and by their false teaching, "caused many to stumble in the law," there is a characterization of the true priest, which presents a beautiful picture of what the faithful ambassador of God and teacher of the people should be. Speaking of a time when the priests and Levites did what was right in His sight, it is said:

"My covenant was with him of life and peace; and I gave them to him *for* the fear wherewith he feared me, and was afraid before my name. The law of truth was in his mouth, and iniquity was not found in his lips: he walked with me in peace and equity, and did turn many away from iniquity. For the priest's lips should keep knowledge, and they should seek the law at his mouth: for he *is* the messenger of the Lord of hosts" (chap. ii. 5, 6, 7).

Here it is declared that, in the time when the priests lived in the fear of the Lord and faithfully declared His statutes, God fulfilled His covenant and gave them "life and peace," and made their ministry a blessing to others. In this comprehensive reference to the former state of things, a flash of divine light is thrown upon the lives of a class of faithful witnesses, of whom nothing is known. In these far-off times, there were among the priests and Levites brave and saintly souls, unknown to earthly fame, who "served their generation by the will of God," and whose unrecorded labors, "turned many away from iniquity." This teaches us that it is not right to base large conclusions on the silence of brief and fragmentary records of distant ages.

There is in these words a lesson for all times. The true minister of Christ is to walk with God in the uprightness of a holy life, and to teach the people, not his own thoughts, but "the law of truth," in which God has made known His will concerning the children of men. Only where these features characterize the ministry of the Word will the result be "to turn many away from iniquity." There is something eminently instructive in the thought that the teacher of the people should be what is here described, because "he is the messenger of the Lord of hosts." The thought here suggests the words of St. Paul to the Corinthians: "Therefore, seeing we have this ministry, as we have received mercy, we faint not; but have renounced the hidden things of dishonesty, not walking in craftiness, nor handling the Word of God deceitfully, but by manifestation of the truth, commending ourselves to every man's conscience in the sight of God" (2 Cor. iv. 1, 2). This implies, not merely that the messenger of the Lord should be a good man, but that his character and testimony should be so blended that the truths he preaches to others shall be minted in the experience of his own heart. This was the secret of the power of the early Methodist preachers, and of all who have preached with spiritual power. What they preached was not abstract theological dogmas, but the living truths of a personal experience. It has been well said: "Doctrine incarnated in character is the most effective way of teaching."

Replies to the Cavils of Unbelief.

A striking feature of this book is the way in which the prophet voices and replies to the unbelieving questionings, by which a disobedient and gainsaying people sought to justify their departure from the ways of righteousness. In these searching replies they " are rebuked for a skepticism that questioned moral distinctions and scoffed at the threatenings of judgment." The light of truth from heaven lays bare their sin and sweeps away the refuges of lies. Denying the goodness of Jehovah, they ask, "Wherein hast thou loved us?" The evidence of this love is shown in the contrast between their condition and that of a kindred nation, and in the way in which they had been crowned with lovingkindness and tender mercy. Resenting the charges of the prophet, they ask, "Wherein have we despised thy name?" The answer is, that they have withheld what was due, and polluted the altar by offering what had defects and blemishes. Instead of the long-suffering of God leading them to repentance, "because sentence against an evil work was not executed speedily," they ask,

"Where is the God of judgment?" Jehovah points to a coming day when the Angel of the Covenant, even the Lord whom they professed to seek, would come in judgment to fulfil what He had spoken; and He declares that it is not because of His unfaithfulness, but because of His unchanging love that they were not consumed.

When charged with speaking against God, they say, "Wherein have we spoken so much against thee?" The answer shows how greatly their disbelief had dishonored God. They had declared that it was vain to serve God or keep His ordinances; and that the proud and wicked were happy and blest, rather than those who served Jehovah. The reply to this bold blasphemy is exceedingly suggestive. They are told, though their sin had so blinded them that they could not discern between the obedient and the transgressor, yet there was among them a people who "feared the Lord and thought upon his name"; and who strengthened each other's faith by frequent religious fellowship, in which they talked together of the things of God. And so far from there being no difference between the servants of the Most High and the disobedient, there is an assurance given that those loyal souls, who in times of degeneracy had "kept the faith," were registered in God's "book of remembrance," and should be His peculiar treasure in the great coming day of trial; and that He "shall spare them as a man spareth his own son that serveth him." And then, even those who had denied that there was any advantage in God's service, shall "discern between the righteous and the wicked, between him that serveth God and him that serveth him not."

In this reply a great admonitory truth is set forth, which is adapted to our day as well as to that time. Sin blunts and blinds the moral perceptions of its slaves. Persons and things appear different in the eye of Heaven from the way they appear to the children of this world. The false judgments, formed in the fogs of unbelief, shall be reversed in the chancery of heaven. They shall shrivel into deformity in the light that flashes from the throne of purity and love. In the day when, as St. Paul expresses it, "the fire shall try every man's work of what sort it is," there shall be terrible awakenings; for those who have not known the awakening of faith must know the awakening of despair.

THE CONVERSION OF THE GENTILES FORETOLD.

In a cursory reading of the prophets, we are apt to think that their outlook was too narrowly confined to Israel, that the brotherhood of man was not recognized, and that the choice of one people to be the depositaries of the divine law and counsels was partial and exclusive. But it should not be forgotten that this election of Israel was not merely for their sakes, but that they should be witnesses and disseminators of revealed truth in the world. "The selection and training of a nation to be a divine agency to make known to the world the knowledge of God, and his glorious purpose for the redemption of humanity by Christ, is a more wonderful and sublime conception

than can be found anywhere outside of the Bible."*
The same principle is seen in God's dealings with
men. The gifts He bestows upon individuals or communities are not partial favors given for purposes of
selfish gratification, but to qualify for service in lifting humanity up into the light and liberty of God.

The prophecies, however, are not all from this narrow, national standpoint. Isaiah and other prophets
obtain glimpses of a time when the forces of the Gentiles shall come in. The local and temporary reference of the Hebrew prophets often becomes the
height from which they behold a broader vision of
universal blessing. But Malachi is the first who
clearly portrays the rejection of the Jews, and the ingathering of believing Gentiles in their stead. Jehovah declares that, because of their wickedness, He
had no pleasure in them, and that He would not accept their offering. Then follows this remarkable
prophecy: " For from the rising of the sun even to
the going down of the same, my name shall be
great among the Gentiles; and in every place incense shall be offered to my name and a pure offering:
for my name shall be great among the heathen, saith
the Lord of hosts." (Mal. i. 11.)

This cannot mean that the idolatrous heathen worship was acceptable to God. It is a prediction of the
results of the all-embracing love that would characterize the Messianic Kingdom. It is the same event
of which Christ spoke to the woman of Samaria,
when He declared that true worship was no longer

*Jesus, the Messiah.

confined to sacred places; but that they who would worship the Father "must worship Him in spirit and truth." Of this prophecy the late Professor Franz Delitzsch says: "Even this one prophetic word makes Malachi one of the greatest prophets."

The Moral Teaching of the Prophecy.

As we have seen, it is not uncommon to hear disparagement of the moral teaching of the Old Testament, as if it conformed to a low ethical standard. Others sneer at revealed religion as something made up of pious feeling and hopes of heaven. An unprejudiced study of Malachi's theology would correct these false assumptions. There is no approval here of a religion that consists in outward observances, which do not affect the character and life. In common with the earlier prophets, the kind of religion here demanded is eminently practical. It deals with the duties of the relations of men to God and to their fellow-men. If it points towards heaven, earthly duties are not forgotten. There is a passage in the third chapter in which the duties of man towards man are presented with wonderful vividness and power. God says: "And I will come near to you in judgment; and I will be a swift witness against the sorcerers, and against the adulterers, and against false swearers, against those that oppress the hireling in his wages, the widow and the fatherless, and that turn aside the stranger from his right, and fear not me, saith the Lord of hosts" (ch. iii. 5, 6).

From the sins that are here the objects of divine

condemnation and threatened punishment, we may learn what is the conduct which God approves and requires. What are the opposite of these forms of sin? Intelligent faith, chastity, truthfulness, just and upright dealing by masters towards servants, and kindness toward all who are friendless and needy. All this is to be rendered in the fear of the Lord. That is, with a constant recognition that we are acting under the eye of our Father in heaven, to whom the rights and interests of His lowliest children are dear. It is often said that the Church shall never have the influence with the toiling masses which it ought to have, until all Christians manifest greater practical sympathy with the rights and interests of that class. Those who maintain this idea may find here a religion that strongly emphasizes this duty. It is instructive to note how all through the Old Testament Jehovah represents Himself as the friend and helper of the oppressed.

These lessons for the conduct of life are unchangingly adapted to the people of all times and nations, because the sinners of Malachi's day are types of sinners that have existed in all ages. In those who questioned and disbelieved the divine faithfulness, and those who rested in outward rites that had lost their spiritual significance, we see the beginnings of the full-blown skepticism and formalism of the Sadducees and Pharisees of our Lord's day. And still, questioning disbelievers who repudiate God's claims on their homage and service, and nominal Christians who substitute outward conformity for the faith and love of the heart, like the poor, we have always with us.

The grounds on which these duties towards God and men are based, like the duties themselves, are of universal application. In the opening words of the prophecy, Jehovah reminds Israel of the great love wherewith He had loved them, as shown in His dealings with them. This has been fitly called the keynote of the book. Even His chastisements were prompted by His loving interest in their welfare. It is said in Amos: " You only have I known of all the families of the earth, therefore I will punish you for all your iniquities." This exhaustless, all-embracing love of God for His creatures claims grateful love in return; and heightens the guilt of the sins that are committed against such infinite fatherly goodness.

Another ground of God's claim to obedience, presented by the prophet, is His relationship to them as Father and Master. They had withheld the honor due to Him as a Father and the fear and obedience due to Him as Master. In this appeal the great truth is suggested that all moral obligations arise out of the relations of being. Not only does duty to God spring from our relations to Him, but that we have all one Father is given as a reason for brotherly kindness and justice between men. The denial of the divine fatherhood dissolves the bonds and obligations of human brotherhood to those who accept such denial. One class of theologians represents God almost solely as a sovereign Ruler; and it is sometimes falsely said that this is the only conception of God presented in the Old Testament. Another class speaks of the loving fatherhood of God, in a way that virtually excludes the idea of justice and moral government. In this prophecy both these attributes are clearly set forth; and any theology that does not fully recognize both is gravely defective.

The Coming of the Messiah Foretold.

I can only refer very briefly to that part of Malachi's prophecy which has attracted the greatest attention, and is most prominent in the thoughts of Christians, when Malachi is named. I mean the sublime prophecy of the coming of the Lord, to be preceded by the coming of Elijah the prophet, who is to prepare the way before Him. No doubt, one reason why this closing prophecy of the Old Testament has awakened so much interest is, because the angel who spoke to Zacharias, the father of John the Baptist, and our Lord Himself, distinctly intimate that this prediction respecting Elijah was fulfilled by the ministry of John.

In studying this prophecy, we may feel at first that the intimations of the coming One and the work of judgment assigned to Him do not completely agree with our ideas of the character of the Prince of Peace, or the actual fulfilment by Christ. The words, "Who may abide the day of His coming?" sound more like wrath than mercy.

This difficulty arises mainly from the blending of the human and divine in the sacred writings. Some prophecies are definite and explicit in their statements respecting coming events. In other cases, the main idea or truth is divinely revealed and firmly grasped by the prophet; but the form of imagery, by which it is expressed by him, has a local coloring, taken from his time and circumstances. We do not believe that the prophet was a mere instrument, through which God spoke words which to him had no meaning; but the way in which God in His providence fulfilled the prophecy is often far higher than the prophet's conception of His message. We make difficulties by giving more prominence in our thought to the Oriental imagery or form, than to the essential reality predicted. This was substantially the mistake of the Jews of our Lord's time. Elijah the prophet did not come as the forerunner; but John came "in the spirit and power of Elijah," and prepared the way of the Lord. There is reason to think that the greatness of John's preparatory work has not been estimated by the Church at its full value.

A close study of the New Testament will show a profounder agreement between this prophecy and the fulfilment than a superficial view would detect. Malachi speaks of the coming of the Lord as bringing blessing or punishment to different classes, according to their character. St. Paul declares that the heralds of the Gospel were to one class "the savor of death unto death," and to another "the savor of life unto life"; and our Lord himself said, "For judgment I am come into this world." John the Baptist seems to have direct reference to the prophecy of Malachi when he says of Christ, "Whose fan is in his hand, and he will throughly purge his floor and gather his wheat into his garner; but he will burn up the chaff with unquenchable fire." (Matt. iii. 12.)

In the concluding chapter, there is this remarkable injunction: "Remember ye the law of Moses, my servant, which I commanded him in Horeb for all Israel, with the statutes and judgments." This explicit reference to the giving of the law by Moses is an important historic testimony. Archdeacon Perowne pertinently says: "A statement like this, put by an inspired prophet into the mouth of God himself, has an important bearing on the historical character and date of composition of the Pentateuch." *

If our observations in this essay have partaken somewhat of the character of preaching, the apology is this: Malachi is so pre-eminently a preacher of righteousness, that to make his prophecy mainly the basis of speculative disquisitions would be out of harmony with the spirit and character of oracles, that are mainly earnest calls to repentance. The notable decline in the character of the Hebrew writings of the times succeeding Malachi, like that which characterizes the Christian literature in the age succeeding the apostles, is an indirect testimony to the divine inspiration of the prophetic writings. It also furnishes an argument against the theory that the Holy Scriptures are the product of a gradual naturalistic evolution.

* Notes on Malachi, p. 38.

No Signs of Prophetic Decline.

I have not spoken of the style of the prophet. It is concise and practical, direct and forcible. He uses pointed interrogation with striking effect. There is no toning down, by the use of euphuistic language, of the stern message he has to deliver. We cannot agree with the school who regard the prophets chiefly as poets, and say that "the language is prosaic and manifests the decaying spirit of prophecy." As Dr. Pusey says, "The poetic form was but an accident." The ability to write poetry is a natural gift. It is in the style that the human element is seen. If the office of the prophet is to convey God's message faithfully to the people, his rank among his fellow-prophets does not depend upon poetic forms of speech; but upon the greatness of the spiritual truths and divine purposes, of which he has been made the revealer and messenger.

Judged by this standard, this last of the Hebrew prophets presents no symptoms of decline. The lofty conceptions of the Divine character presented in this prophecy—the profoundly spiritual ideal of the worship and service which God requires—the insight and power with which the excuses for prevailing sins are unmasked—the magnificent prediction of the establishment of Christ's kingdom among the Gentiles—the unfaltering courage with which wicked men in high places are rebuked—the wonderful adaptation of the moral teaching of this prophecy to all times—the comprehensive conception of religion as a principle governing all the relations of life—the broad prophetic light shed upon the coming of the Messianic King of Righteousness—all vindicate for Malachi a high and enduring place in the "goodly fellowship of the prophets," by whom God has made known His will to the children of men.

X.

IS THE WORLD GROWING WORSE?

THERE can be no question that our moods, or the eyes with which we look at things, largely determine the impression they make upon us. Everything looks bright to glad and hopeful hearts. On the other hand, the desponding and sorrowful clothe all things in the hues of their own sombre spirits. Many people maintain that the world is going from bad to worse. The aged are apt to look back upon their youth as a vanished golden age. It is an article in the faith of one theological school that the world shall continue to grow worse, till the second coming of Christ ushers in the millennium.

There is much more fault-finding and grumbling in the world than thanksgiving and praise. Apart from all theological theories, there is a general disposition to disparage the existing condition of things. Some people find fault with everything that is being done in both Church and State. No matter how well anything is done, they can point out "a more excellent way." Their gaze is so constantly fixed on failures and blemishes that they overlook the signs of progress around them. It is with reluctance such people admit that there is any real religious growth or improvement in the world.

There are natural causes which go far to account for the prevalence of this pessimistic tendency. The ills of life touch us more closely than its blessings. They are always with us in some form. The prick of the thorn causes a far keener sensation than the beauty and fragrance of the rose. Much of the grumbling is done under the pressure of some passing ill. The great majority of people are not happy, and unhappy people are always complaining people. In times like the present, when the echoes of Armenian massacres are in the air and Christian nations are brandishing the sword, expressions of opinion are apt to be colored by the dark shadows of the hour, without fully recognizing the progress of bygone peaceful years.

It is also undeniable that every one who adopts a new theory or fad, on any social or religious subject, feels bound to disparage and condemn all existing beliefs or practices which stand in the way of the acceptance of his theory. For this cause it is necessary that we know what people believe, before we ascribe any importance to their approval or condemnation of things. The infidel condemns the Christian religion as something worthless or mischievous, unworthy the acceptance of intelligent men. Roman Catholic writers wax eloquent over the failure of Protestantism, and especially of Protestant missions, without much regard to the actual facts. In 1850 Archbishop Hughes asserted that "Protestantism had lost all central force and power over the masses of mankind." High Church priests who have adopted the Romanist conception of the Church and the ministry also pronounce evangelical Protestantism a failure. Many years ago, the Rev. Dr. Ewer of New York, a ritualistic Episcopalian, said that Protestantism was "a broken raft" falling to pieces in a stormy sea. Rationalists, who reject the belief that the doctrines of the Bible are a supernatural revelation from God, consequently regard the religion that rests on this belief as too unscientific for this scientific age. All these, in whatever they may differ, agree in disparaging the work of evangelical Christianity in the world, and in making confident assertions that the facts justify their dark view of things.

I firmly believe that the hopeful feeling produced by confidence in the "faith once delivered unto the saints," greatly promotes earnestness in Christian work. I also believe the facts of Christian history show that Christianity has vindicated its adaptation to the wants of the children of men, and contributed largely to political, social and religious progress. It may conduce in some degree to strengthen the faith and zeal of others, if I briefly state some of the reasons why I believe that these pessimistic views are not justified.

It will hardly be denied by any one that there has been great progress in useful knowledge during the past century, and that a great increase in the physical comfort of the people has followed as a result. It is not a mere coincidence that mental and material advancement has gone on side by side with religious progress. In many cases the latter has been evidently the cause of the former. Doubtless those who are looking for evils and wrongs, with which to make a dark picture, can always find material enough suitable for that purpose; but beyond all question the past hundred years has witnessed great religious progress. No writer known to me has treated this whole subject so ably and fully as Dr. Daniel Dorchester, in his book "The Problem of Religious Progress," of which a revised edition was published by Hunt & Eaton, New York, in 1894. Dr. Dorchester quotes fully and fairly some of the strongest pessimistic statements of skeptics, Romanists and Ritualists; then, by an unanswerable array of authentic facts and statistics, he proves that the indictment of Protestantism by its enemies is false and faulty. He presents the multiplying evidences that "Christianity is more and more penetrating the world's consciousness and life, and demonstrating her efficiency as a regenerating and uplifting power among the nations."

It would take too much space to state in detail the historic facts by which this conclusion is sustained. I can only briefly name some of the signs of moral and social progress seen in modern times, especially in English-speaking countries. Among these are greater independence and liberty of thought—the passing away of crude and unscriptural statements of doctrine — the prevalence of a higher standard of moral conduct — the diminution of crime—the growing temperance sentiment—a purer and higher tone in popular literature—the discontinuance of duelling and the disbelief in witchcraft—the more humane treatment of women and children—greater practical sympathy with the toiling poor—the multiplication of benevolent institutions for all classes of sufferers—more ample and efficient provision for popular education—the removal of barbarity in the infliction of judicial penalties—the overthrow of slavery in the British dominions and the United States—increased interest in missionary success—increase in spiritual vitality in all the Protestant Churches—a large and steady increase in the membership and agencies of the Protestant Churches in the United States and Canada—the deep and widespread influence of religious literature—the greater interest shown in the religious education of the young—the enlarged sphere and influence of woman—the concentration of thought upon the Bible—and a more liberal and fraternal spirit between different denominations of Christians.

These and other indisputable signs of progress, which are amply demonstrated as facts by Dr. Dorchester, constitute an overwhelming body of evidence that, notwithstanding some adverse facts and occasional times of reaction, the Christian Churches evince undoubted religious progress—a progress which proves that evangelical Christianity is exerting a powerful influence upon the world. The wickedness, injustice and moral degradation which exist in Christian lands do not result from any inefficiency of Christianity; but from the neglect or rejection of the salvation it offers and the duties it enjoins. The contrast between the social and religious condition which prevails at the present time and that of the last century is striking and eminently encouraging. Roman Catholics disparage Protestant missions, yet the success of Protestant missions during this century more than equals that of the primitive Church during the first century. Modern missions also have had their days of Pentecost. "In a single year, one missionary society received eighteen thousand seekers after the truth; another baptized nine thousand converts, six thousand in one day; and another received six thousand to membership." But missionary success cannot be measured by the number of converts received into the Churches. At the Chicago "Parliament of Religions" it was quite evident that men who represented the heathen religions were familiar with Christianity, and were largely indebted to it while they disparaged it. The way in which Christianity has triumphed over powerful enemies in the past, and the evidence that it is still the power of God unto salvation to every one that believeth, should strengthen our faith in its divine efficiency, and prompt us to more earnest effort in bringing our unsaved fellow-men at home and abroad to a saving knowledge of the truth.

XI.

THEOLOGY IN THE PUBLIC SCHOOLS.

THE intimate relation which the education of children sustains to their future character as citizens invests the instruction they receive during their school life with more than ordinary interest and importance. School life is a miniature forecast of the larger life of manhood and womanhood. Its difficulties, tests of character, and elements of success, are substantially the same as those of mature years. As the drill of a soldier, that does not fit him for actual warfare, would be pronounced a wrong method, so if the education which children receive at school is not adapted to make them good citizens, it fails in its main purpose.

In formulating an educational scheme, we must have due regard to the actual conditions of things in the country for which it is intended. A system that might answer for a mission school, or for a country where all the people were of one religious faith, would not be practicable in a country like ours, where there are different Christian Churches possessing equal rights. There are only three possible systems. One that provides for denominational schools, or one that provides for united moral and secular teaching, or purely secular schools. I regard the united education of the children of the people as a most desirable thing, that cannot be lightly given up. There are two strong objections to any educational system which divides the people on Church lines: (1) Such a division of the children of the people into denominational sections, by dividing up these sources available for school purposes in the different districts, would greatly weaken the schools and lessen their efficiency. (2) An equally serious objection is, that such a system tends directly to create sectarian lines of separation, inimical to patriotic unity in political and municipal affairs. The demand for denominational schools, in order that the religious faith of a particular Church may be taught to its children, is a virtual declaration that the religious beliefs of all other Churches are so erroneous as to render this separation necessary. Such an assumption cannot fail to create prejudice, in the minds of those who believe this, against their fellow-citizens of a different religious faith. Those who are unitedly to carry on the affairs of the country in the future should be educated together. But sectarian theological teaching in the schools, no matter under what pretext it is introduced, tends directly to prevent this desirable unity of all denominations in the public schools of the country.

It will be generally admitted that any education which does not embrace moral and religious culture is radically defective. We may differ as to the agency by which such culture is to be given, but there can be no difference as to its vital importance.

Intellectual acuteness and intelligence alone are not a sufficient equipment for the duties of life. Dr. Lyman Abbott, in an article in the *Century Magazine,* remarks that, "if it is the primary right and duty of the State to give whatever education is necessary for good citizenship, it is self-evident that it is its primary right and duty to give education in moral principles, and training to the moral impulses and the will." He further says: "The men who are to determine what are the rights and duties of the State in dealing with other States, what are the rights and duties of the individual citizens in dealing with one another, what is the nature, penalty and cure of crime, and what is the moral quality of the corporate and co-operative acts of the community, are to determine moral questions, and must be educated to perceive moral distinctions, and to see that moral considerations always outweigh considerations of mere expediency or apparent self-interest. Nor is it possible to give such moral instruction and training without involving something of the religious spirit, if not of religious education."

With these sentiments, I confess I am in substantial agreement. I believe that moral and religious training is as essential to qualify for useful citizenship as the acquisition of knowledge and the development of the intellectual faculties. I would, therefore, approve of such moral and religious training in the public schools as may be given, without coming into collision with the religious convictions of the parents who make up the constituency of the schools. While there is so much ethical and religious truth held in common by all Christians, I cannot see why it should be impossible to unite in a practical recognition of those common religious principles that bear on character and conduct.

But this general inculcation of religious duty should be carried out more by the spirit and conduct of the teacher, and the way in which discipline is administered, than by formal theological instruction. The public schools of Ontario and Manitoba are probably as near what public schools ought to be as is practicable in the present condition of things. Lessons on moral conduct might be added with advantage. I do not agree with those who think the reading of a portion of Scripture and the offering of prayer are too small a thing to be worth contending for. There is in this simple exercise a recognition of the divine authority, which is adapted to make an enduring impression on the minds of children.

Though I hold strong views as to the importance of religious education, I have no sympathy with a good deal that is said in favour of religious teaching in the public schools. It is frequently assumed, that if the children are not taught theology in the public school, they will be left to grow up irreligious and immoral. This notion throws discredit upon the work and influence of the Christian Churches. The public services of the churches, the teaching in Sunday-schools, the abundant supply of religious literature, and the influence of Christian home life should not be thrust out of sight as if they were of no account, in order to magnify the importance of doctrinal teaching in the school. As a matter of fact, if you take the godly men and women of any church, and inquire by what human agency they were brought to a saving knowledge of the truth, you will find that only an infinitesimally small proportion of them would ascribe their religious character to instruction received in the school. Neither is there any satisfactory evidence that the children educated in church schools present a higher type of moral character than those educated in national schools. The assumption that all increase of crime is evidence that there is a wrong system of training in our public schools is not justifiable. This crime may take place in spite of the influence of the schools rather than as a result of their teaching. At any rate, it may as forcibly be charged against the churches, which exist avowedly to teach morality and religion, and yet have failed to extinguish crime.

The teaching of church creeds in Government schools involves the principle of the union of Church and State—that is, of the State choosing a religion for the people, and applying public money to pay for teaching such religion. This is something which the Protestants of this country will not approve except, as in the case of this Province, a formal agreement renders it obligatory to make a special concession on this point.

The loudest demand for religious teaching in the schools is generally made by those who desire to have the peculiar doctrines of their creed taught, rather than sound Christian morals. The demand is almost always sectarian rather than religious. This is seen in the case of the Roman Catholics. While they condemn unsectarian public schools as irreligious and immoral, the most thorough biblical and moral instruction in the schools would not satisfy them, unless the dogmas of their Church are taught, under the direction of their clergy.

The same thing is seen in the zeal for doctrinal teaching shown by the High Church party in England. Under the plea of zeal for religion, they are now pressing the Salisbury Government to reward their Church, for the help given in the recent election, by a large grant for Church schools. The London *Speaker*, in a recent issue, says:

"It is in the name of religion that they make this outrageous demand, and they try to bolster up their cause by appealing to the natural feeling of their fellow-countrymen in favor of the training of our children in the faith of their fathers. We are willing to admit that they are perfectly sincere in thus confounding the cause of religion with the cause of a particular denomination. That is the common error of all sectarians. But it is obvious that this country many years ago decided formally that the funds of the State should not be employed in teaching the dogmas of any particular Church, and that we should violate this great Constitutional principle, established in the first instance by the Liberal party and long since accepted by the Tory party, if we were now to yield to the clerical demands. Furthermore, it has been made abundantly clear that if once we agree to permit dogmatic teaching at the public expense, we cannot draw any line that will effectually limit the dogmas taught. We shall have to pay for teaching doctrines which are most directly opposed to each other, and which are not only repudiated but detested by those who are forced to contribute to the cost of spreading them."

It is extraordinary that at a time when the claims of Church schools in England are calling forth the strongest protests from Nonconformists and causing extensive strife and irritation, any Canadian should point to the sectarian schools of England as something that should help to reconcile us to sectarian schools in Canada. England has many undesirable things, like the crooked streets in her quaint old towns, that have grown so and cannot well be changed now. But it would be folly for us, who are free to build as we deem best, to copy what must be regarded as blemishes and hindrances to progress, rather than laudable things worthy of imitation.

I am aware that it may be said that even the moderate unsectarian degree of moral training which I have approved, may be the occasion of conscientious objections to some parents. Well, in all such cases the school authorities must decide whether the complaint is just and reasonable or not. If any parent objects that what is taught to his children is untrue or wrong, his objection should receive due attention, whether his judgment be deemed right or not. No child should be subjected to any religious instruction to which its parents object. But an objection to a school, because the doctrines of any Church are not taught in it, does not deserve the same consideration. If any unbeliever objects to his children receiving Christian teaching, his wish should be duly regarded. But such a one has no right to demand that the order of the school, or the law that enjoins it, should be framed according to his particular belief. The conscience of the minority should be duly protected against any violation or infringement; but no minority of the people have any right to demand that their views, and not those of the majority, should be embodied in the public policy of the country.

It may possibly be said, that the religious and moral lessons or exercises, which I have approved, are open to the objection of involving the principle of the union of Church and State. I do not think so. We should not make a bogey of State Churchism, in a way that would require Governments to shut out of consideration all moral distinctions. The chief objection to a State Church is the unjust bestowment of favors on those who hold one form of religious belief and worship. In a country where an overwhelming majority of the people profess the Christian faith, I do not think the recognition of those principles and moral precepts of Christianity that are held in common by all Churches can be justly regarded as State Churchism. So long as there is no selection of a sectarian religion for the people by the State—no application of public money for the teaching of the doctrines of any Church—no interference with liberty of conscience—and no favor shown to any section of the people because of their religious belief, there is no good ground to complain of State Churchism.

I am utterly opposed to a State Church. Yet I do not admit that opposition to State Churchism makes it the duty of a government or parliament, which represents a Christian community, to make no distinction between the principles of Christian morals and the views of atheists, pagans and agnostics.

But I am free to confess that if such united religious teaching as seems to me desirable and proper should prove impracticable, I would rather give up all formal religious teaching in our public schools, than accept a system of denominational schools; because I believe this would be a greater evil than the absence of direct religious teaching in the schools. I would, however, remind Christian people who volunteer to completely secularize our public schools, that they probably do not see how far this may carry them. The principles of Christian faith and morals are woven into our history and literature. The demand for secularizing the schools may be so urged as to mean a good deal more than omitting the reading of the Scriptures and prayer. Secularization may be interpreted to mean the exclusion of historic facts and essential ethical teaching from our school books, on the ground that they are Christian, and therefore sectarian. Besides, nothing is gained by secularizing the schools, so far as the Roman Catholics are concerned. Secular schools are just as objectionable to them as the so-called "Protestant Schools" of Ontario and Manitoba. What they demand is "Separate Schools," in which their religion will be taught to their children, under the direction of their clergy. Right moral conduct should be enforced, and a reverent spirit promoted in our schools and colleges; but it must be admitted that our public schools are not, for several reasons, the best agency for teaching theology and religion to our children. The agitation for denominational teaching in our public schools is an assault on the unity and efficiency of our educational system.

LATER POEMS.

WRITTEN SINCE THE PUBLICATION OF "SONGS OF LIFE."

THE LONG VICTORIAN REIGN.

With pealing bells and every flag unfurled,
   We hail the grandest reign that earth has seen;
And British freemen, belting the round world,
   Shout with one voice, "God save the Queen!"

All hail, Victoria, though enthroned on high
   In the "fierce light" throughout thy peerless reign,
Thou canst through all the watching world defy
   To point to blameful blot or stain.

The queenliest Queen of all the starry ages,
   Wise, faithful mother and true, loving wife,
Thy reign has graved on our historic pages
   A pure and noble woman's life.

From every colony, from land and main,
   From distant islands of the sounding sea,
There come the echoes of one glad refrain
   Of grateful, loyal love to thee.

Not Greece or Italy or sovran Rome,
  In all the splendor of their pristine days,
Had half the glory of thine island home,
  Or deeds so worthy deathless lays.

Not battles bravely fought on land and sea,
  Where Victory crowned and widened British power;
Not the vast empire Heaven has given to thee
  Calls forth the joy of this glad hour.

The growth of liberty, the spread of truth
  Which brought new life to many a lowly lot,
Opened the gates of knowledge to our youth,
  And gave new wings to human thought;

Science that wrung from ocean, air and earth
  Secrets to lighten toil and soften pain—
Reforms that broke the gyves from honest worth
  And lifted manhood to a higher plain:

These are the glories of Victoria's reign,
  The grateful pride alike of age and youth,
Who prize above all martial fame or gain
  Freedom and righteousness and truth.

We love her for the sorrows that she knew,
  Her tender sympathy where grief was sore,
The trusting faith that kept her heart so true
  To God and duty evermore.

June, 1897.

TO THE CANADIAN NIGHT-HAWK.

Mysterious watchman of the night,
    Keeping lone vigil in the sky,
Though silent through the hours of light,
    And dim thy dazzled eye,

Soon as the twilight shadows fall,
    With open eye and tireless wing,
Thou dost obey some mystic call
    To soar aloft and sing.

In boyhood I have often stood
    And watched thy circling flights as here;
A little clearing in the wood
    Was then thy narrow sphere.

I deemed the forest wild thy home,
    Thy solitude evoked my pity;
I knew not then that thou wouldst come
    To watch o'er town and city.

Why dost thou not with gladsome lay
    Salute the opening morning hour,
Or sing farewell to fading day
    In tree or leafy bower?

Thy day is night; while others sleep
    Thy monotone is heard on high,
As if it was thy joy to keep
    The freedom of the sky.

A mystery I cannot solve,
   The purpose of thy toil make known ;
Why in these circling rounds revolve
   And sing all night alone ?

Art thou a spirit doomed to bear
   And suffer for some mystic crime,
Upon this treadmill in the air,
   A penal term of time ?

Is thy shrill note a pitying wail
   Over the misery that lies
Concealed, beneath night's shrouding veil,
   From gaze of human eyes ?

Or is thy chant a note of gladness
   For peaceful rest which night imparts—
The brief release from toil and sadness
   Of worn and weary hearts ?

Like many a toiler in the field
   Of life, no good seems wrought by thee ;
Yet all true work shall fruitage yield,
   Which now we cannot see.

The meed of gold or words of praise
   Which human hearts with zeal inspire,
To spur thee on or prompt thy lays
   Thou never dost require.

Despiser of the world's acclaim,
   This lesson in my heart enthrone—
For right and truth, unheeding blame
   Or praise, to stand alone.

Toronto, 1897.

ON THE DEATH OF LORD TENNYSON.

The brightest star in Britain's sky of fame
   Has passed beyond the range of mortal sight ;
But on the hearts of men a deathless name
   Is graved in characters of golden light.

The Bard whose peerless songs of life and love
   Have charmed the ills of hearts by care opprest,
Has "crossed the bar"—is havened safe above,
   Where life is love and service joyous rest.

We render thanks, not tears or mournful lays,
   For him who with a manly, stainless life
Filled up the circle of his lengthened days,
   And nerved his fellows in their fateful strife.

Beauty and truth unseen by other eyes
   His touch unveiled and clothed in living fire ;
Nature's unuttered music found a voice
   In the sweet tones of his melodious lyre.

The knightly souls of Albion's mythic youth
   Upon his page live o'er their lives again :
His seer-like thought reflects the light of truth
   On the great problems of the heart and brain.

He loved Old England ; of her glory proud
   Her weal and woe were of his life a part ;
Oft as his bugle-blast rang clear and loud,
   It stirred the blood in every patriot heart.

His ashes rest with England's kings of song ;
   But his freed spirit chants a loftier strain,
And his great thoughts and scorn of selfish wrong—
   His truer self—shall evermore remain.

Though ocean spreads its wide and stormy sway
   Between us and the land he held so dear,
These maple leaves in grateful love I lay
   With English roses on his honored bier.

Toronto, October, 1892.

THEN AND NOW.

A Supplemental Response to Lord Tennyson's "Locksley Hall Sixty Years After."

Though the poet peer of England, in a sad despondent strain,
Sings of dark and baleful evils which o'ercast the people's reign,
Men of hopeful faith forget not how our century has outgrown
Cruel wrongs and heartless customs that were once on fashion's throne.

Why in every clime and period have the fearful and the old,
Glorified the vanished ages as the Eden age of gold?
Change and progress, larger freedom, which the tide of time has brought,
Are but signs of blight and ruin, by the rash and reckless wrought.

Forms of life and truth must vary with the spirit of the years;
Fairest blossoms of the springtime wither ere the fruit appears.
Every age moulds thought and action by its free and living mind—
Should we cast away the kernel for the roughness of the rind?

When the hopes of youth are buoyant, and the pulse of
    life keeps time
To the glad inspiring music of love's melodies sublime,
All the world is bathed in brightness; hope pours balm on
    every smart;
And the bleakest scenes are goldened by the sunshine in
    the heart.

When the fires of life burn dimly, and the false and self-
    ish world
Chills our hopeful trust and courage till the flags of faith
    are furled,
Then the world without grows darker; things which once
    seemed good and fair
The despondent spirit colors with the hues of its despair.

Looking backward through the ages of which timid croak-
    ers boast,
They are black with wrongs and falsehoods, that are now
    a vanquished host;
For the "good old times" embosomed brainless follies,
    social crimes,
That we would not brook a moment in these kindlier, better
    times.

Who that shares the light and freedom, which like blessed
    sunlight falls
On the peasant's lowly cottage freely as on lordly halls,
Would go back to times of darkness ere the sun of freedom
    rose,
And renounce the wealth of blessing which this latest age
    bestows?

Then the vast and mystic forces God through nature had diffused
Were, alike by sage and savage, undiscovered and unused :
Now these powers, like living creatures, have been taught by human skill—
Wear man's yoke and bear his burdens, faithful servants to his will.

Learning then was Fortune's favor, to the poor by fate denied :
Now the gates of Truth and Knowledge unto all stand open wide ;
And the poor man's boy, with only honest heart and active brain,
May evince his native kingship and the highest place attain.

Then the toiling and the lowly were each petty tyrant's scorn,
Doomed to stay with dumb submission in the sphere where they were born :
Now the sons of toil are honored, while their selfish despots cower ;
For the voice of honest Labor has become a voice of power.

Then the multitude, unthinking, blindly drank the potion given ;
Took the words of human teachers as the very words of Heaven.
Only few with faith and courage Truth herself supremely prized,
While the slaves of custom worshipped what the past had canonized.

Now o'er Truth's vast sea exploring, Thought's free pennons are unfurled;
There's a mental resurrection like the springtime of a world.
Creed and teacher must be tested as by fire in fiercest light;
For the question of the age is, "IS IT TRUE AND IS IT RIGHT?"

Law, so long the rich man's weapon, keeping pelf and power secure,
Now extends its strong protection to the feeble and the poor.
Lonely souls through other ages wrought and battled in the van;
Now the range of deeds heroic spans the brotherhood of man.

THEN, like soulless beasts of burden, men and women bought with gold
Were by heartless Christian brothers into life-long bondage sold;
Now through every clime and country rings the jubilant decree,
That, in spite of race and color, every human soul is free.

Christless multitudes, unpitied, down to deeper thraldom swept;
Left alone in guilt and darkness while the Church supinely slept;
Now to every tribe and nation, where God's name was never named,
Messages of free salvation are with living power proclaimed.

Is it right, because past evils do not thwart our present aims,
To make light of them and cover cruel wrongs with pleasant names?

And to slight the fruits of freedom, now to rich and poor supplied,
Which through all those vaunted ages were unrighteously denied?

Why bewail the strife and struggles that disturb this restless time,
As the signs of coming chaos, which presage decay and crime?
All the cherished light and progress that have lifted up the race
Have been won by throes and conflicts which to better things gave place.

Picture not as Sons of Anak, every wrong that Truth must slay;
You can win no crown of triumph dreaming dreams that breed dismay.
Faithless doubt will crush the courage that the victor strength imparts;
We must face life's ills and conflicts with unquailing, hopeful hearts.

Brood not over stormy passions surging round some chronic wrong;
High above the noise of battle Faith may hear the victor's song.
Toil yields rest and beauty blossoms from a dark, "unsightly root;"
Summer's sourness holds the promise of the Autumn's ruddy fruit.

In the lives of men and nations, comes no crown of bliss supreme
To the stolid and slow-hearted who have floated with the stream.

Hottest fires of painful trial, heavy burdens, fiercest strife,
Lift the struggling spirit higher, nerve and beautify the life.

Men who meekly cringe and pander to advance some cherished cause,
May be counted wise and prudent, win the shallow world's applause;
Yet I'd rather brave its hatred, standing lonely in the fight,
And be loyal to my conscience and to what is true and right.

Ignorance, Injustice, Folly, linger still, while myriads wait
Till the valleys are exalted and the crooked paths made straight.
But the direst ills and follies which becloud the world to-day
Are but shades of darker evils that have almost passed away.

Doubtless Prejudice and Passion may unthinking crowds unite;
And the blind may lead the blind while they trample on the right;
Bitter feuds of creeds and classes find no cure in human code;
In true and Christly brotherhood, men must bear each other's load.

Rough and steep the path of progress; slowly earth's oppressions die:
Yet the world is rising higher as the burdened years go by.
Truth and Righteousness, unconquered, in this warfare shall prevail;
This the God of Truth has promised, and His Word can never fail.

Toronto, 1888.

OUR DEAR DEAD BOY.

In Loving Memory of Albert Ernest Dewart, who died suddenly on the 9th of January, 1877, aged 5 years 1 month and 12 days.

He beamed upon our path of life
   Like golden star from heaven,
Gilding Earth's dark and toilful strife
   With hopes as blessings given ;
A type of all things fair and bright,
Whose love gave rare and sweet delight.

A blossom on the brow of Spring—
   A limpid, gladsome stream—
A bird that sang on joyous wing—
   A love-sent, sunny beam,
Which Christ-like calmed the waves of care,
And made life beautifully fair.

His love, like blessed sunshine, fell
   Upon Earth's wintry gloom ;
And in each bleak and cheerless dell
   Made flowers of hope to bloom.
He knew not that his soft caresses
Had peerless power to cheer and bless us.

But Death has hushed our song-bird's strain—
    The gladsome stream is dry;
The star that brightened gloom and pain
    Has vanished from our sky;
The sweetest blossom in Love's bower
Has withered in life's dewy hour!

I left my blue-eyed boy at morn,
    Without a shade of fear
O'ercasting heart or brain, to warn
    Of fateful danger near;
And in a few short hours he lay
A pallid, lifeless form of clay.

I reel beneath the sudden blow—
    And yet, though hope has fled,
My heart cannot believe its woe—
    I cannot think him dead—
Nor that this loving heart of thine
Shall never more respond to mine!

At times I think the struggle o'er;
    I strive to trust and pray—
Then comes his image back once more—
    I hear his voice at play,
And chide my heart, as if it slept
Upon the sacred watch it kept.

When wailing winds o'er vale and hill
    On wings of darkness ride,
It startles with a piercing thrill,
    To think our joy and pride,
On whom such wealth of love was shed,
Lies cold and silent with the dead.

OUR DEAR DEAD BOY.

I close my eyes in dream-like thought,
   And trace with mournful joy
The form and features, ne'er forgot,
   Of our sweet angel boy.
That cherished vision still shall be
Dear as a glimpse of heaven to me.

He still is with us, not less dear;
   Our love shall ever shrine
A mystic, loving presence near
   His mother's heart and mine:
In spite of Death, through all life's hours
Our darling Albert still is ours.

Around his name sweet memories throng;
   His childish toys bring tears:
And sweeter than a seraph's song
   Each hymn he loved appears:
All that recalls our dear, dead boy
Gives sorrow thoughts akin to joy.

Yet, not in vain the gift was given,
   Though brief his stay below,
He was a teacher, sent by Heaven
   Love's deathless power to show.
Our chastened hearts through loss shall gain
A keener sympathy with pain.

Oh, blissful thought! thy gentle breast
   Shall feel no aching pain:
No storm can break thy tranquil rest,
   No sin thy spirit stain;
No sigh of grief—no tears shall flow
For ills that darken life below.

Father, forgive our tears and grief;
    The stroke is hard to bear;
No earthly power can give relief,
    Or brighten our despair.
Take Thou our trembling hands in Thine;
Soothe earthly grief with balm divine.

Shed light upon our darksome path,
    Thy needed grace impart;
And teach us, though it seems like wrath,
    How merciful Thou art.
From bitter seeds of grief and gloom
Let flowers of faith and patience bloom.

Teach our faint hearts to trust Thy love,
    Through Sorrow's darkest night;
And wait till—in the world above
    Where Death can never blight—
Forever safe from grief and pain,
We meet our darling boy again.

Toronto, January, 1877.

DEATH OF JOHN KEATS.

JOHN KEATS, a young English poet of the last generation, was not at first appreciated at his true worth. His poems were so severely criticised in *The Quarterly Review,* that Shelley and others speak of this as the occasion of his early death. There is, however, no reason to doubt that he suffered from a constitutional tendency to pulmonary consumption, of which he died. "Endymion," "The Eve of St. Agnes," "Hyperion" and other poems were published in London, before failing health caused him to go to Italy in 1820. He was accompanied by a young English artist friend, named Severn, who was among the few who had formed a high estimate of his genius. The poet's health failed rapidly, and he died in Rome in 1821, at the early age of twenty-five years. During his last illness, Severn attended him faithfully and tenderly ; and when he died laid him in a grave in the Protestant cemetery in Rome, of which Shelley said, "It might make one in love with death to think one should be buried in so sweet a place." Shelley's own ashes were buried there, not much over a year later. At Keats' own request the words, "Here lies one whose name was writ in water," were inscribed on his tombstone. Not only has Keats taken high rank as a poet of most original genius, but his poetry has exerted a marked influence on the poets of a later generation. He is the poet of poets. No poet had produced works of greater promise at the same age. Severn spent his whole life in Rome, and was buried at last in the same cemetery as Keats and Shelley. A recent visit to Hampstead, London, where Keats lived and wrote before he went to Italy, and the commemoration of the centenary of his birth on the 29th of last month, led me to resurrect the following unpublished verses, written many years ago in the flush of my early admiration for Keats. Of course, the reference to Severn's being buried in the same place as Keats has been added on a recent revision.

Toronto, November 21, 1895.

Fast sinks the youthful poet. Death has set
   His seal upon his fair and classic brow :
The light of genius lingers on it yet ;
    The friends beloved are distant from him now,
      Who sang, in words to be forgotten never,
      "A thing of beauty is a joy forever."

The hand that sweetly swept the tuneful lyre
   Is trembling in the icy grasp of death ;
Chill'd are the pulses of poetic fire,
    And swiftly fails his feeble, fitful breath,
      A lowly grave upon a foreign shore
      Shall yield the rest which earth ne'er gave before.

No mother's form bends o'er his dying bed,
   No sister's hand allays his wasting pain ;
But light and love from heaven itself are shed
    On him who ne'er shall sing on earth again.
      Unseen angelic spirits hover there
      To waft to heaven the dying poet's prayer.

No, not alone—one kindred soul is near
  To minister in life's sad closing hours—
To whisper words of holy hope and cheer,
  And solace give as death's dark shadow lowers;
    Severn keeps watch with Sorrow's wistful eyes,
    While in life's morn a priest of Nature dies.

O, not in water didst thou write thy name,
  Sweet bard! Thy graphic verse, so full of love
And beauty, vested with a deathless fame,
  Its magic power o'er human hearts shall prove,
    And ruthless Time's corroding power defy—
    Immortal Keats, thy name shall never die!

Rome keeps his dust, though prouder tombs are there,
  Where conquerors lie and lofty temples shine,
Yet oft the sons of Albion shall repair,
  As reverent pilgrims to a sacred shrine;
    And kindred hearts with silent sorrow weep
    O'er that sweet spot where Keats and Severn sleep.

LINES TO A PESSIMIST.

Forbear these pessimistic wails and growls,
And limit not thy thought to pictures dark
And painful. Doubtless life has gloom and grief,
Bleak sunless hours of bitterness and pain,
When every star of hope is hid from sight.
Failure and falsehood often deeply pierce
The trusting soul with sorrow's poignant shafts;
But these pain-giving ills unseal the heart
To kindlier sympathy with human woe.
Their reign is brief. Life has more day than night,
More genial summer calms than wintry storms.

Say not that sorrows fill the larger space
And give their color to the web of life.
The sombre tints are often in the eyes
With which we look at life and earthly things.
We paint in colors furnished by dark moods,
And ills we dread are shadows of ourselves.
Along our roughest paths grow plants and flowers,
Which yield a healing balsam for our woes.
Our transient hours of sorrow are outweighed
By friendship's countless, kindly ministries.
Children's affection, true and unalloyed
By hateful shadows of distrust and pride,—
The bliss ineffable of trusting love,—
The tenderness of mother and true wife,—
Are founts of pure joy-giving happiness,
Which temper the chill blasts of wintry fate.

LINES TO A PESSIMIST.

The grand and beautiful in Nature's fanes
Are wordless preachers to grief-smitten hearts;
They bear sweet messages of peace for all
Whose ears are open to their healing tones.
The glorious sunrise, vesting hills and vales
In garniture of radiant golden joy,
Making the world a vision of delight,
Betimes has chased the shadows of distrust
And made a gladsome sunshine in my heart.
The primal forest, an Eolian harp
On which the winds play lays of freedom,
Where choirs of singing birds proclaim their joy—
Our crystal lakes studded with isles of green,
Broad sheets of burnished silver, giving back
The floating clouds and stately margin trees,
Have hushed the murmurs of a fretful mood
And shed a tranquil calm o'er brooding care,
Of which the memory is a joy untold,
Which gives forth light in lone and darksome hours.

The massive mountains, on whose towering peaks
Eternal snows and fleecy clouds unite
To weave a gleaming ermine robe, above
The flashing glaciers which adorn their sides,
And the abysmal gorges at their feet
Where brawling rivers madly rush and rave,
Or dark blue lakes slumber in sheltered peace,
Have spoken with a voice divine of His
Almighty power and changeless faithfulness,
Who built the everlasting hills which stand
As earthly emblems of His unseen throne.

But grander far than mountain, lake or sea,
The wondrous thought, that the Eternal One,
Whose wisdom, power and love are infinite,
Through all the darkness and the strife of time
Is working out His vast and wise designs.
We may not pierce the shrouding veil, until
The daybreak of Eternity shall dawn ;
Then heaven's unclouded light shall show to all
That Sorrow was the minister of Love,
And all Earth's painful ills and problems dark
Unsightly seeds which yielded golden fruit.

CHRISTMASTIDE.

At Christmastide we wistfully turn
   Our thoughts to the years that are past,
To joys that are ashes in memory's urn,
   And we grieve that they could not last.

What hopes we cherished in life's gay prime!
   What castles we built in the air!
Which the iron hand of pitiless Time
   Has covered with shrouds of despair.

A pictured vision breaks clear on my sight
   Of faces that beamed with love and glee—
And voices that thrilled with rare delight,
   And were sweetest music to me.

The dearest friends of those Christmastides
   Passed away with the years that are fled:
Beautiful maidens and hopeful brides
   Now are wrinkled and gray, or dead.

Yet with silent force these vanished years
   Have moulded our life and thought;
And they live anew in the deeds we do
   While we count them as things forgot.

Though the friends and hopes that gave joy in youth,
   Now seem like a dream that is told,
We can welcome the Christ and trust His truth
   As we did in the days of old.

THE SONG OF THE WIND.*

Ye spirits of air, so potent and fair,
  That roam through the starry sky,
Follow my flight on your pinions light,
  For who is more mighty than I?
Like you, I sweep through the liquid deep,
  Invisible, swift and strong,
And gladness or woe dispense as I go,
  With gentle or terrible song.

When the scorching blaze of the summer's rays
  Its burdensome languor brings,
I silently fan both beast and man
  With my cool invisible wings.
I carry the rain from the distant main,
  Like a patient servant of toil,
And fling it in showers o'er the drooping flowers,
  And the sunburnt, thirsty soil.

To the fevered cheek of the faint and weak
  A grateful joy I impart;
And in sultry hours, with the breath of flowers,
  I gladden the weary heart,
When the earth is cold, and the winter grows old,
  I bring the warm breath of spring;
And my power is felt, when the ice-chains melt,
  And the rivers in concert sing.

* This is an abridged version of the poem published in "Songs of Life."

THE SONG OF THE WIND.

I breathe through the trees, a musical breeze—
   On my wind-harp, the forest, I play ;
When I pass in the storm, wearing terror's form,
   Then the forest kings bow to my sway.
I rend the oak with the whirlwind's stroke,
   Or play with the thistledown ;
When I sink to sleep the blue heavens weep,
   And the silvery dews come down.

When the heavens are dark, and each golden spark
   Is mantled from mortal view,
I scatter the clouds, those starry shrouds,
   And open the boundless blue.
With favoring gales, I fill the sails
   Of the vessels that plow the main,
Till the sailors rejoice, with merry voice,
   When they reach the haven again.

I strip the leaves from the forest trees,
   And scatter them far and wide,
Till they spangle the plain with color and stain,
   As fair as in summer's pride.
I madly blow the fresh-fallen snow,
   And pile it in glittering heaps,
Till the hillocks rise, to fancy's eyes,
   Like the grave where a giant sleeps.

O'er the mountains high, which are lost in the sky,
   I skip with an airy tread ;
But the midnight hour is the time of my power,
   When the snowy carpet is spread ;
Then in doleful shrieks the night-wind speaks,
   To summon the demons of air ;
And there seems a strife as for death and life,
   Which is followed by groans of despair.

When the ocean vast hears my trumpet blast
    Roll over its bosom wide,
Then up from the deep the billows leap,
    In their fierce, untamable pride.
On the rocky shore their sullen roar
    Fills the mariner's home with dread;
For there comes a wail upon every gale,
    As sad as the voice of the dead.

When I sweep in wrath on my briny path,
    The vessels my might who brave,
With their precious freight, yield to merciless fate,
    And are buried beneath the wave.
And they weep on the land, the deeds of my land,
    In many a sorrowful dwelling;
But my stern heart can know no pity for woe,
    When the tide of my ire is swelling.

Over land, over sea, still tireless I flee,
    Like my guardian spirit, the sun;
The day may go, and the night may flow,
    My labor is never done.
Neither sun nor rain, which ripens the grain,
    Brings gifts more precious and rare;
For life and health are the priceless wealth
    That my breezy zephyrs bear.

None of mortal birth—no monarch of earth—
    Has an empire so grand and wide;
Since the birth of time, over every clime
    I have swayed my sceptre with pride.
And yet, though I sing with the pride of a king,
    And boast of my boundless sway,
His servant am I, who ruleth on high,
    Whom the winds and the seas obey.

IN MEMORIAM
WILLIAM EWART GLADSTONE.

A MIGHTY nation mourns her greatest son,
   Who bore the torch of progress in the van.
Leader of men, thy great life-work is done—
   Reformer, Patriot, Sage, and Friend of Man!

Not only Britain mourns; from every land
   There come sad tones of blended grief and praise,
For him who with unquailing heart and hand
   Stood for the right through all his lengthened days:

A giant oak among the forest trees,
   Strong to resist the fiercest storms that blow—
An eagle soaring till the sun he sees
   And heralds brighter day to earth below.

Not on the gory fields of martial fame
   His deathless deeds of chivalry were wrought;
The glory that surrounds his starry name
   Was won by battles in the realms of thought.

A man of peace, he life-long war maintained
   That justice might oppressive wrongs displace;
The triumphs which his knightly valor gained
   Were all to bless his country and his race.

To freedom's Land of Promise, rich and fair,
   With peerless eloquence of tongue and pen,
Through seas of strife and deserts of despair,
   He made a pathway for the sons of men.

His words were swords, which cut the Gordian knots
   Of partial laws that long held dire control;
But greater than his potent words and thoughts
   The human sympathy that filled his soul.

When throned in lofty place of power and fame,
   On that high stage he played a noble part;
To-day the voices of the world proclaim,
   His highest place was in the people's heart.

By faith in God the power to him was given
   To move right on, nor swerve for friend or foe;
He ever brought the light and strength of heaven
   To do the work of earth for men below.

There's nothing in the star-lit heavens above,
   Nor earth beneath in all her summer glory,
More beautiful than manhood, truth and love,
   Wrought out and carved in deed and living story.

The name of Gladstone shall forever shed
   A guiding light on the high path he trod—
A grand heroic soul in heart and head—
   True to himself, his country, and his God.

Toronto, May 20th, 1898.

Works by the Same Author

Jesus the Messiah. In Prophecy and Fulfilment. A Reply to Dr. G. C. Workman on Messianic Prophecy. Cloth, 256 pages, net 35 cents.

Dr. J. W. Mendenhall, Editor of the *Methodist Review*, New York, wrote of this work:

"This is a triumphant book—triumphant in its defence of the historic opinion of prophecy, and triumphant in its exposure of the weakness and rationalistic character of negative criticism. Necessarily controversial, being incited by Professor Workman's extreme positions, it is singularly free from a narrow partisanship and is transparently fair in its representation of opposing views. . . . It is written in a charming style, and exhibits the mature strength, the sagacity and reflecting power of a very capable and influential writer."

Songs of Life: A Collection of Original Poems. Cloth, 75 cents.

Living Epistles; or, Christ's Witnesses in the World. Cloth, 75 cents.

The Development of Doctrine. 10 cents.

High Church Pretensions; or, Methodism and the Church of England. 10c.

Broken Reeds, The Heresies of the Plymouth Brethren and other Evangelists shown to be contrary to Scripture and Reason. 10 cents.

Waymarks; or, Counsel and Encouragement to Penitent Seekers of Salvation. 3 cents.

Misleading Lights. A Review of Current Antinomian Theories of the Atonement and Justification. 3 cents.

WILLIAM BRIGGS, Publisher
29-33 Richmond Street West, - - TORONTO

IN PREPARATION

The Bible and Higher Criticism

www.ingramcontent.com/pod-product-compliance
Lightning Source LLC
Chambersburg PA
CBHW020924230426
43666CB00008B/1566